THE STORY OF SHEFFIELD AT WAR
1939 TO 1945

THE STORY OF SHEFFIELD AT WAR 1939 TO 1945

MARGARET DRINKALL

Pen & Sword
MILITARY

First published in Great Britain in 2016 by
Pen & Sword Military
an imprint of
Pen & Sword Books Ltd
47 Church Street
Barnsley
South Yorkshire
S70 2AS

ISBN 978 1 47383 361 6

A CIP catalogue record for this book is available from the British
Library.

Typeset in Plantin by
Mac Style Ltd, Bridlington, East Yorkshire
Printed and bound in the UK by CPI Group (UK) Ltd, Croydon,
CR0 4YY

Pen & Sword Books Ltd incorporates the imprints of Pen & Sword
Archaeology, Atlas, Aviation, Battleground, Discovery, Family
History, History, Maritime, Military, Naval, Politics, Railways,
Select, Transport, True Crime, and Fiction, Frontline Books, Leo
Cooper, Praetorian Press, Seaforth Publishing and Wharncliffe.

For a complete list of Pen & Sword titles please contact
PEN & SWORD BOOKS LIMITED
47 Church Street, Barnsley, South Yorkshire, S70 2AS, England
E-mail: enquiries@pen-and-sword.co.uk
Website: www.pen-and-sword.co.uk

Contents

Acknowledgements   vi
Introduction   vii

Chapter 1   The Countdown to War   1

Chapter 2   The Civil Defence of the City   13

Chapter 3   The Evacuations   24

Chapter 4   The Sheffield Home Guard   38

Chapter 5   The First Air-Raids   56

Chapter 6   The Sheffield Blitz   71

Chapter 7   Later Raids   91

Chapter 8   Sheffield Women at War   102

Chapter 9   The Sheffield Police at War   119

Chapter 10   Bombed-Out Families   141

Chapter 11   Eminent Visitors to the City   151

Chapter 12   The Americans in Sheffield   170

Chapter 13   Peace at Last   183

Sources   198
Index   199

Acknowledgements

All authors owe a debt of gratitude to those who have assisted them along the road of research in sourcing valuable quotes, archive materials, images from the period and in all manner of other ways. Therefore my list of appreciation is fairly comprehensive and I am indebted to all the following.

My most grateful thanks go out to an anonymous gentleman who, at a book-signing in the Rotherham Visitor Centre, brought a book to show me. The book in question was *Sheffield at War* which had been brought out sixty-eight years previously by the *Star* newspaper. When I told him that was the subject of my next book, he generously gave it to me, while at the same time refusing to tell me his name.

I also wish to thank Rob Hollingworth, the managing editor of the *Star*, for permission to use many of the photographs from the book, which are priceless (and as the images have been obtained from the same source, their captions have not been individually credited). I would like to also offer my thanks to Brian French, who very kindly gave me a copy of *Charlie's War*, the war diary of Charles Simms, a former Sheffield councillor and JP. No local history book could be written without the most generous help of the staff at both Sheffield and Rotherham Archives. I would also like to thank Matt Jones and Pamela Covey of Pen and Sword, whose skilful editing makes sense of my ramblings, and Mat Blurton and Jon Wilkinson for their exceptional book and cover designs. I wish also to acknowledge the help given to me by my son Chris, whose skills in photography and IT still amaze and confound me. Without all of you, this book might never have been written. Finally, I would also like to acknowledge my nephew Oliver Patrick Galvin, who sadly died during the completion of this book. Requiescat in pace, Ollie.

Introduction

Almost from the beginning of the Second World War, the government and the city authorities knew how crucial Sheffield's main industry of steel production would be to the enemy. They knew that the Vickers works would be a target because of a 15-ton drop-hammer, which for the first eighteen months of the war was the only machine in the country able to produce Rolls Royce crankshafts for Spitfire and Hurricane aircraft. The hammer was so important that it was in constant use for sixteen out of every twenty-four hours, working seven days a week. Sheffield was also the site of Hadfields Steel Works, which were essential for producing 18in armour-

The 15-ton drop-hammer at the Vickers Works.

piercing shells. They knew, without doubt, that consequently the city would be directly in the enemy's firing line. What they underestimated was that the Germans would bomb the city and its people indiscriminately and not stick to the targeted industrialized areas.

By using contemporary extracts from documents, diaries, accounts and letters, I hope to illustrate just how much suffering the Sheffield people went through during the war years. These items reveal the many concerns brought about by war, and the alarm engendered by the bombings. They also record the real fear of invasion that was prevalent at the time. Even the police records contained advice on how officers were to behave, should the enemy invade. Yet they also illustrate the positive side of the people who showed determination and great courage in the face of adversity. However, there are too many individual tales of heroism and bravery shown by ordinary people to record fully here, particularly during the bombings of December 1940. There have been many books written about the devastation that became known as the Sheffield blitz, although none concentrate on the other air-raids that took place from 1940 to 1942. No other books record the fact that Sheffield police were involved in the training of British secret agents, or how crucial the housewives of Sheffield were to the development of radar. There is also little record of the GIs that came to the city, although their stay was both an attraction and a deterrent. I apologize in advance for the terminology used when reporting the activities of the Americans in the city and the use of language that would certainly not be acceptable today. However, for the sake of authenticity I will use such quotes as they were given in order to illustrate the way in which certain sectors of the population were viewed at the time.

CHAPTER ONE

The Countdown to War

To look at the columns of the local newspapers in the summer of 1939, there appears to be little evidence that another war was imminent. The *Sheffield Telegraph and Independent* of 22 July merely report that the city's steel output of the previous six months had increased by 15,200 tons, which was said to be the highest record of any year. The *Star* pointed out the 'Glories of the Countryside within easy reach of Sheffield', listing Hathersage, Castleton and Lathkill Dale in Derbyshire from as little as 2s 8d return. Those local people who did consider any forthcoming hostilities desperately hoped that appeasement would prevent warfare. In September 1939, even the local councillors were optimistic. While opening the Woodsetts Church fête, Sheffield Alderman E. Dunn MP

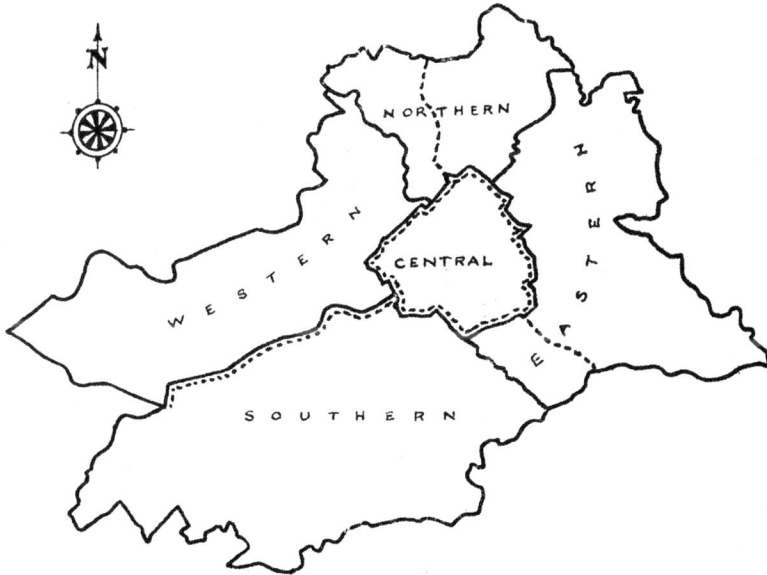

The divisions of the City of Sheffield used by police and the civil defence services.

told the crowd that 'I do not think the international situation is as precarious as it was a year ago, but I could not say that the danger has passed.'

Nevertheless, like the rest of the country, Sheffield was making preparations for war as early as October 1938 with the creation of the ARP (Air Raid Precautions) Emergency Committee, led by Councillor W. Asbury. At the inaugural meeting it decided that for administrative purposes, the city would be sectioned into the five areas already in use by the police force. Each section – north, south, east, west and central – would have a control and a report centre. The committee was well aware that if war came, the greatest danger would be from the air and their immediate concern was to build air-raid shelters to protect the populace. Many discussions took place on how to provide as much blast-proof accommodation as cheaply as possible should hostilities break out. The committee decided that each local employer would have to be responsible for the safety of their workforce and to this end they caused questionnaires to be sent out to each person employing more than twenty men. The questionnaire asked what cellars could be used, not only for the workmen but also for the public at large. From this information they found some suitable industrial accommodation that could be used for both large and small groups of people. However, the committee decided that even with a minimum outlay, the cellars available could not offer enough protection for the whole population of the city.

The discussions continued and by May of 1939 the need for air-raid shelters was becoming more urgent. That same month, the city engineers approached the owners of large buildings and offered to strengthen the basements with sufficient space free of charge. These basements would provide safety for large numbers of people caught in the city centre streets during air-raids. As well as the strengthened basements, trenches made of concrete had been dug in many of the city parks which were opened immediately for public use. By June 1940 more of these trenches were to be found in playing fields, parks and golf clubs throughout the city. These served the dual purpose of not only providing protection from air-raids but also preventing the landing of enemy aircraft. The defence of the city had been made such a priority that by August 1939 the chair Councillor Asbury announced to the press that 'Sheffield stands supreme throughout the country in air raid shelter accommodation.' He added that there were now air-raid shelters sufficient for over 51,000 people who found themselves stranded in a raid. He added that more public shelters were under construction that would hold another 11,000 people, making 62,000 altogether. It had been decided that the master keys for the shelters were to be kept in the possession of all wardens and police constables when they were not in use. Spare keys were kept in cases near to the entrance of the shelters, in small illuminated boxes to which members of the public could break the glass in times of danger.

Enrolment into the civil defence services was also put in motion and the committee organized for cards stating 'I am willing to serve' to be offered in places of entertainment around the city. Newspapers carried requests for people to join the wardens, the ARP and the AFS (Auxiliary Fire Service) which were fairly successful. It was reported on 12 May 1939 that 15,278 people had volunteered out of a total of 20,313 that were needed. Sheffield's Chief Warden, Captain Clement Roberts, assured

Captain Clement Roberts, Chief Warden of Sheffield.

a reporter that 'All air raid wardens could now be brought into action in a matter of moments, and that everything was prepared.' Some 400 of these early volunteers were used as enumerators in the census that was carried out in Sheffield. More than 100,000 identity cards were issued for individual townspeople. Each card contained two warnings: firstly, that every person had to be responsible for preserving their own card; and, most importantly, that they must be kept with that person at all times. Individuals were warned that they must not pass the identity cards on to any unauthorized person or stranger.

Britain was convinced that this second world war would include the use of gas bombs. As a result of this, the Emergency Committee minutes made a request for 568,000 gas masks from the government in August 1939, one for each of its citizens. The gas masks were actually delivered the following month and were the first batch to be delivered from the government stores in London. However, when they arrived it was noted that no tools had been delivered with them and consequently they could not be assembled. Finally the tools were delivered and on 26 September the Home Office authorized the Corporation to assemble and distribute the respirators. The work proceeded by day and by night, which included opening thousands of boxes containing face-pieces and the rest. In total, 487,150 respirators were soon ready for distribution. Arrangements were also made for gas vans to tour the city on a regular basis to test the respirators and these became a familiar sight to many people. It was announced on 25 October 1939 by Councillor Asbury that gas mask distribution would be in effect within the next few days. He warned the people that the names of the distribution centres would be given out by the press and people were to collect them from there.

At this point in time little thought had been given to protecting children under the age of 2 from gas attacks, although on Wednesday, 30 August 1939 a demonstration was given using a 6-month-old boy called Johnny Vernon at the Court House in Sheffield. When the mask was placed over the little boy, he submitted patiently to the ARP worker. Head wardens and deputies watched carefully for any signs of distress as it was placed over his head. It was reported that 'He neither kicked nor screamed; he merely glared through the window of his helmet at a uniformed policeman and nonchalantly sucked his thumb.' So it was not until Monday, 11 September 1939, after war had been declared, that gas masks for children were quickly issued from fifty-eight distribution centres. Councillor Asbury reminded the people of the city that the respirators were the property of the government and must be given up on request.

By February of 1939 it was agreed that steel Anderson shelters, named after Sir John Anderson who initiated their development, would be distributed by the government to those living in the areas of Sheffield that were at most risk. These would be delivered by the local authority to many of the householders who had no cellars available and had no other form of protection. The erection and positioning in the garden of such shelters would also be supervised by the local authority. The government announced that it was the duty of every house-owner to make provision for shelter accommodation for himself and his family. A government pamphlet titled *Your House as an Air Raid Shelter* was produced to illustrate how people could turn their house into a place of safety. By February of 1940 it was thought that the defence of the city of Sheffield and its inhabitants was nearing completion. It was announced in the leaflet entitled *Emergency Committee for Civil Defence in Times of War* that over 59,000 Anderson shelters had been delivered for distribution.

As well as having to ensure that there was adequate shelter for the population of Sheffield, in March 1939 the Emergency Committee was preparing to deal with the blackout. That month a national appeal had been received in Sheffield to 'take all precautions to ensure that street lighting could be extinguished at a moment's notice.' The committee ensured that staff would be standing by, ready to make all necessary adjustments to traffic signals and bollards immediately, should the need arise. Arrangements were also made to ensure that all lights in the town centre shops could be switched off as soon as an air-raid warning was given. The committee warned householders that they must take the responsibility of ensuring that they had plenty of emergency lighting for their homes in the form of torches and candles. At what was described as 'one of Sheffield's largest stores' people were already buying portable lamps and window blinds, blackout curtain and adhesive tape for covering up all windows and doors. Blackout restrictions were also imposed on the traffic. The city engineer had teams of men working night and day to make the streets safer for drivers by painting white lines in the centre of roads and marking out pedestrian crossings.

Air-raid siren on the roof of Sheffield City Hall.

Covers were placed over traffic lights and only small crosses were visible to drivers.

Several sirens were installed on various roofs in Sheffield such as the Weston Park Museum and City Hall. A test was made of the siren at 8 pm on 20 August 1939 and another the following night. In case there was any ambiguity about the sound of the sirens, it was announced in the local newspapers that in the event of an air-raid, electric sirens would issue a warbling note. There would also be intermittent blasts on the steam sirens, which would be augmented by wardens riding bicycles riding through the city blowing their whistles. Other wardens carrying hand rattles would indicate the 'all-clear' signal and a steady note by the sirens would be given once the raiders had passed. On Friday, 25 August 1939 a reporter from the *Sheffield Telegraph and Independent* went out into the city to see for himself how the population was dealing with the possible impact of war. He reported that throughout the streets there was a general calm and when he stopped members of the public, he found that many people refused to be down-hearted. One, who he described as a working man from Tinsley, told him 'If war is going to happen it will happen and there is no point in worrying about it, but personally I do not think it will happen.' He found that most people were optimistic about the future, 'whether they were road workers, business men or housewives.' Yet even at this late stage, even with all the preparations having been made, he said that many refused to believe that there would be a war. He wrote that people continued to carry on with their normal everyday lives, not showing any worry or panic. He also noted that in the local shops most people were buying food items, whereas shops selling furniture or toys had found their sales almost at a standstill.

On Saturday, 26 August 1939 a headline in the local newspaper reported that 'Sheffield gets on with its Emergency Plans' as it outlined the emergency drill for workers leaving their machines in order to get to the air-raid shelters. The firm of Messrs Thomas Firth and John Brown were tested as to how long it would take the 6,000 employees to leave the works. It was intended that the same tests would be carried out in all their plants including those at Norfolk and Atlas Works. A local reporter attended one of the demonstrations and stated that:

I have today watched a mass evacuation of one of Sheffield's munitions works and the courageous attitude of the employed there has impressed me. The works are in the industrial heart of the city, but I saw there was no sign of fear or nerves. I have been deeply impressed with the high morale and the willingness of the people to do whatever they can for National Service.

He also stated that he had interviewed one elderly woman, who had been with the firm for thirty years, who remembered the bombs being dropped on Sheffield in the First World War. She told him that in those days there had been no provision for shelter from the bombs. Now the local firms had provided well-built air-raid shelters that were comfortable and roomy with a purifying plant providing fresh air.

Despite the fact that no evacuation orders for the children had been received by May 1939, the Emergency Committee discussed how it should be carried out. It had been decided that the evacuation would come under the auspices of the Education Committee and a plan was established that the Chief Education Officer would organize a dummy run. It was agreed that 'The practice evacuation of the children will take place on 28 May.' The exercise with the schoolchildren was successfully carried out and the Education Committee reported that Sheffield was ready to evacuate 30,000 children on the first day that war was declared.

On Sunday, 27 August 1939 Sheffield people did not know it but it was to be the last week of peace they would know for the next five years. A reporter visited an armament works to talk to some of the workers there. He said that although the factory was situated in the centre of the city, there was no sign of fear or nerves. He enquired if any of the workers were thinking of leaving their jobs in order to move to industries in safer areas. He received an emphatic 'no' in return. As one worker explained: 'Our work is part of National Service.' A woman who worked there optimistically told the reporter: 'Anyway the German planes will never be allowed to get as far as Sheffield – and why worry, there is not going to be a war.'

By Tuesday, 29 August preparations had been put in place to protect the city archives. All the city's important records, manuscripts, valuable books and the special collections were now safe in strong underground rooms. Newspaper files going back to the eighteenth century had been placed in the library basement, although it was reported that the art gallery had no plans in place at that time to preserve their own collections. A reporter from the *Star* newspaper was told that there were 310 different wardens' posts in place in Sheffield and all of them were operational. Each post was virtually the nerve centre for the section in which it served. He reported that he 'had learned today that the members of the ATS [Auxiliary Territorial Service] would not be called up until there is a general mobilisation on the outbreak of hostilities. Nevertheless the members in Sheffield are standing by in readiness.'

By Thursday, 31 August the news that everyone had been dreading had arrived and now no one could pretend that war was not imminent. Notice was given by the town clerk on behalf of Sheffield Council that the Lord Privy Seal had directed that 'the emergency machinery for war was to be put into motion.' The local gas companies assured the Emergency Committee that they were building duplicate plants to ensure that if the supply was disrupted, the other plant could be utilized. The two plants would be some distance from each other and they had been suitably camouflaged. Steps had also been taken to remove the name of the city from the top of the gasholders in order to protect it from enemy aircraft. A representative of the Edison Swan Electric Light Co. told a reporter that the side streets of the city would not be lit at all for the foreseeable future. He said that 'The public are asked to accept the inconvenience which will be caused, and to recognise that this step is taken as one of the preparations which are necessary in the case of a sudden air raid.'

The chief of Sheffield Fire Brigade, Superintendent C. Teather, stated that several special tanks each containing 5,000 gallons of clean water had been put all over the city to be used as an emergency supply if needed. He also requested another 400 volunteers for the AFS which he hoped to increase to 2,000 men.

On 1 September 1939 it was announced to the Emergency Committee that the city of Sheffield was now ready for war. Councillor Asbury told them that the air-raid wardens' preparations were now complete and the city could go onto a war basis at any moment if necessary. A special depot was opened for those civilians who still had not been given their gas masks and it was reported that there was a plentiful supply available. Messages asking for the immediate attendance of the Sheffield Territorials were flashed onto cinema screens and such was the haste that many left to join their unit without being able to say farewell to relatives. A reporter described the scene in the city centre. He said that morning a few spectators watched as one of the huge emergency water tanks was erected and filled in Barker's Pool. Across the road, under the underground car park of the Grand Hotel, the sandbag-filling machine was in operation and men were churning out full sandbags for use around the city. He reported that 'All in all, it seemed that in Sheffield business as usual seemed to be the motto of the man in the street.'

Finally on Sunday, 3 September Britain declared war on Germany. The next day Councillor Asbury told a local reporter that the populace of the city had received the news of the impending war calmly and quietly. When the announcement had been made, many Sheffield people were attending a service in the cathedral. It was not until the end of the service that the prime minister's statement had been relayed to the congregation and special prayers were then held. Within fifteen hours of the PM's declaration, Sheffield had its first experience of war conditions when in the early hours of the morning of 4 September the warning sirens were sounded. Due to the amount of preparation beforehand, the people of Sheffield were fully organized. They simply went to the safety of the shelters as quickly as possible where they remained until the all-clear sounded. It was later said to be a valuable exercise as people discovered from the experience the urgent need to keep gas masks and torches near to their beds. The few people who were already abroad in the streets when the siren went off had no difficulty in finding the public shelters.

The cathedral, where many people were attending services on 3 September 1939.

The rehearsals for the evacuation of the munitions works that had been held at Hadfields Ltd had also paid dividends. When the alarm sounded, everyone on the night shift stopped their machines and went to the safety of the shelters. Once again it was reported that there was no panic and at Brown Bayley's steelworks the story was the same. The response of the people of the city to the siren was reported to have been 'magnificent'. The English Steel Corporation told the local newspaper that the police had been perfectly satisfied with the complete blackout at the works, which was achieved within minutes of the air-raid warning.

By this time a pamphlet had been distributed to every household telling them what to do in case of an air-raid. This, combined with posters throughout the city, urged householders 'if they are in the house when the siren goes off, to stay there.' They were told that if they had an Anderson shelter or a basement to enter it immediately. Anyone out in the street when the sirens went off should go to the nearest public air-raid shelter. In a foreword to the pamphlet the Lord Mayor, Alderman W.J. Hunter, warned:

> In any period of crisis the man or woman with self control is an asset beyond price. We had all hoped and worked to prevent war, now however it is upon us. It is the duty of every one of us to prepare ourselves for the struggle. This leaflet is issued to help each householder to realise what he can do to make his home more safe against air attack. That can only be done by being prepared for anything which may come. It is essential to show in advance just what it is most necessary to do in an emergency and so avoid panic.

The leaflet then gave instructions on what to do if a fire broke out in a furnished room, the effects of gas on a population and also the effect of the weather if gas bombs had been dropped. The mayor promised householders that if they studied the leaflet carefully they would learn what to do if they were in the streets at a time when they were contaminated by gas and what equipment they should have ready in the home. He assured them that Sheffield Corporation was endeavouring to do everything it could to protect the people of the city and their families. Urging calmness, Alderman Hunter told them when spending time in one of the communal shelters to sing community songs, play a musical instrument 'or do anything which will keep your spirits up and drown any noise outside.' Concluding, he reminded them that 'The enemy is trying to dislocate our civil life and so it is our duty to get on with our lives in the normal way, in spite of the air raids.' Sheffield was now prepared for war.

CHAPTER TWO

The Civil Defence of the City

It was noted on the same day that war had been declared that Sheffield had overnight become a city of sandbags. They were being used to protect civic buildings, cinemas and shops as well as the valuable stained-glass windows in the cathedral. A reporter noted that the only people on the streets were groups of men and women reading notices that had been put up on public buildings. There was almost an unreal feeling as life continued much as before, trams and buses continued to run, and people went out on ordinary Sunday visits to relatives and friends just as on any other weekend. Nevertheless, the great national events had changed everything. The next morning on Monday, 4 September it was announced that the recruitment offices on Surrey Street had been found to be too small. Subsequently recruitment would continue at the larger premises of the Town Hall and the Employment Exchange on West Street. The man in charge of recruitment was Major W.H. Griffiths and he told a reporter that skilled men were needed

The stained-glass window of the cathedral that had to be protected by sandbags.

who had some expertise in engineering and mechanics as well as those who had a good knowledge of radio for the armed services. Now people flooded to enlist in the army, navy and air force. By the end of the day more than 500 applications had been received and by the end of the first week that total had reached over 900 applications. By February 1940 the total number of Sheffield men who had registered for the armed forces was between 16,000 and 17,000 and it was also noted that most applicants wanted to join the RAF. When the men

Charles Simms' signing-on card.

enlisted they signed a National Service Grade card, which men like Charles Simms referred to as the 'signing-on card'.

All the new recruits for the military services were trained in drill before being sent for more technical training. A reporter who visited a training depot for the RAF in September 1939 reported back that he had watched ordinary men of the city being turned into Aircraftmen (2nd Class). He watched as the squad of men paraded at the receiving centre, dressed only in vests and shorts, who had 'walked out of civvy street less than a fortnight earlier.' Their ages were from the middle twenties to thirties but he claimed 'it was difficult to pick out the young from the old.' The centre trained men for every branch of the RAF from balloon operators to bomber pilots, but when they arrived they all received the same initial treatment. Within a matter of days they were transformed from John Smith civilian to A/C2 John Smith RAF. The daily timetable during their training consisted of the following:

6.30 am reveille. Wash, shave and dress
7–7.30 am breakfast
7.30 am cleaning up
8 am first parade and drill
10.20–10.40 am break
10.40 am noon drill
noon to 1.15 pm dinner
1.15 pm parade
4.30 pm tea

After tea on four days a week there were lectures lasting for about an hour. From then until roll call at 9 pm the men were free to do what they liked before lights out at 10.30 pm. During the evening the men had use of the canteen, billiard room, reading and writing room, and the camp cinema that gave shows seven days a week. When the men finished their training, they were passed out by the wing commander and then by the station commander. Finally they received their clearance certificates before being sent on to the appropriate school or station where they would be further inducted into their chosen service.

On the day after war had been declared, the Lord Mayor of Sheffield, Alderman Hunter, addressed the people of Sheffield and he told them that:

Now that we know that a state of war has been declared between this country and Germany, it behoves the city of Sheffield to prepare in every way for what might prove to be the greatest struggle in the history of our Country. At this time of extreme urgency every able-bodied man and woman will be required to do their bit. The liberty, justice and stability of Britain have made this Empire great. These things are our life, and we must defend them with all we have. Sheffield is ready I feel sure, to play a loyal and vital role in the struggle.

He also warned all Sheffield householders that blackout restrictions had now been imposed. If they had not already done so, they had to ensure that their houses were in complete darkness from sunset to sunrise. Shops in the city reported that the demand for cloth for blackout curtains had been huge and a large firm of tailors told the local newspapers that they had sold more than 15,000 yards already. Thankfully they had managed to secure another 50,000 yards, which would be on sale the following morning as soon as the shop opened. The mayor also reminded the people to always carry their respirators with them wherever they went.

For some time before the war the Sheffield steel industry had been preparing for expansion, so when war was declared the city was quickly able to turn its vast resources into making armaments. Now steel was needed for ships, guns and planes, as were armour-plated sheets for tanks. Many steel companies turned their factories into munitions works and within days were working twenty-four-hour shifts. Once war had been declared, younger men working at the many steelworks were needed for the military and as a result hundreds of former Sheffield steelworkers came out of retirement. Within a few months it was reported that they were 'as happy as sandboys' to go back to work. They were thrilled by the thought that they were helping to give Hitler 'one in the eye' for spoiling their retirement. Mr H.F. Walker, the secretary of the Sheffield branch of the Amalgamated Engineering Union, stated that many of the men had been retired for more than five and ten years and were now back in the works. He said:

> We are very proud of our old men for they have answered the call to duty again with commendable patriotism. They are just

Armour-plated sheets for tanks were made in Sheffield.

as proud to do their bit as the lads in uniform. The fact goes unchallenged that our old men are just as determined to play their part in stamping out the Nazis as are the soldiers, sailors and airmen.

The swiftness with which the city responded to the call for arms did not go unnoticed. *The Times* recorded that 'The speed at which Sheffield is furnishing material for the maintenance of our Navy and Army is unprecedented.' Munitions factories flourished in both large and small workshops and it was estimated at the beginning of the war that there were more than 200 steel-making firms in Sheffield alone. Some of these included the English Steel Corporation, the United Steel Company, Viners Ltd, Edgar Allen and Co., Arthur Balfour, Firth Vickers and many others.

Now that a state of war existed some families took to sleeping in the Anderson shelters most nights, using deckchairs and blankets for beds. However, as time went on many of them were turning their shelters into miniature bedrooms. Bunk beds for the Anderson shelters were being advertised and were reasonably priced at £2. The manufacturers claimed that they were easy to install. They were described as being 'a very presentable piece of furniture, with their smart tapestried covering and dark painted woodwork, the bunks should be of considerable use after the war for extra guests who may stay unexpectedly.'

Alternatively, quilted sleeping bags were also on offer that fastened with tapes at the side and they came in all sizes, including special ones for babies. As an example, the following month it was reported that Sapper George D. Mount had successfully altered his parents' Anderson shelter to comfortably sleep four persons. His mother told a local reporter that he had come home on leave in July and almost immediately set about improving the shelter that his father had erected in the back garden. He made the bunks, which were about 16in wide, from stout wood and reinforced sacking, and his mother made four small mattresses out of one large double one, which could be taken out and aired. Sapper Mount installed electricity so they then had lights and an electric heater. Boxes containing food and hot drinks were placed under the bunks when the shelter was in use. Mrs Mount told the reporter that her husband, son and two daughters had slept in the shelter for the last week and they had been very comfortable.

One area of vulnerability identified by the Emergency Committee was the reservoirs above the city. It had been noted as early as 20 September 1939 that something needed to be done in their defence. The committee asked the town clerk and the general manager of the Water Department to enquire how they could protect the city when moonlight shining onto the shape and cluster of the reservoirs would give away the proximity of the city to enemy bombers. Also there was the fear of damage arising from a possible breach in the walls of the reservoirs of the Langsett and Bradfield valleys. However, at that time there was little that the Emergency Committee could do. Much later in April 1943 Wing Commander Guy Gibson, the leader of 617 Squadron RAF ('the Dambusters') trained over the reservoirs of Langsett, Underbank, Ewden and Strines. They were practising with the new 'bouncing bomb' invented by Barnes Wallis in order to breach the Möhne, Eder and Sorpe dams of the heavily-industrialized Ruhr valley. These bombs were dropped from very low-flying planes, and in order to protect the same thing from happening at Sheffield drastic measures had to be taken. Large lattice-framed masts over 300ft high were erected on the vulnerable side of the dam, suspending steel cables across the water. From these hung a vertical curtain of cables that reached down to the water, preventing bombs being dropped from low-flying aircraft. There was also a smokescreen installation implemented that within seconds could flood the areas around the reservoirs, hiding them from enemy aircraft. The Emergency Committee, along with other civil defence services, also took precautions against the reservoir being breached by devising an elaborate evacuation scheme if the signal 'dams breached' was ever given.

In order to co-ordinate the ARP services in the city, regular training exercises replicating the effects of an air-raid were held. It was well-known that in their bombing raids the Germans used incendiary bombs dropped from specially-equipped aircraft that would light up the intended targets. Then a second wave of aircraft would make a concentrated attack on the illuminated

Wire screens and cable protecting the Strines Reservoir from attacks from low-flying aircraft.

areas below and high-explosive bombs would be dropped. One of the main tasks of the civil defence services was therefore to put out the incendiary fire as soon as possible using a stirrup pump, covering it with sand or dirt and smothering the flames. One such exercise was held on Friday, 26 January 1940 involving 2,000 wardens as well as first-aid and civil defence personnel and auxiliary fire-fighters. A signal was sent at 0750 hours to let the people know that a raid was imminent, although the raid did not actually start until 1505 hours. Certain 'incidents' were prepared in advance to illustrate the results of both incendiary and high-explosive bombs being dropped on the city. For their part the AFS tackled fires in several parts of the city, while the ARP services rescued dummy casualties buried in damaged buildings. Live casualties wearing armbands giving details of their injuries were also used. They had to be picked up and taken to first-aid posts where their injuries could be treated. Nearly seventy of these casualties were dealt with at various sites across the city. One exercise involved a bomb dropping on a garage at the bottom of Woodsetts Road that had been set on fire. The wardens 'discovered' the fire at 2030 hours and the fire brigade, with no previous knowledge of the incident, was summoned from Sharrow Vale Road headquarters. They arrived at 2040 hours and the first hose was playing on the 'fire' just four minutes later. Everything worked with precision and organization. Captain Roberts, the chief warden who later received an MBE for his services in 1941, told a reporter: 'Basing my opinion on what has happened tonight, and at other exercises we have held recently, I am certain that Sheffield ARP are ready for every eventuality.'

By the beginning of February 1940 there was an ARP control room whose position was a top-secret matter. The book *Sheffield at War* suggests that the room was situated in the bedrock under the Old Town Hall, which at this time was manned on a twenty-four-hour basis. Others state that the Secret Ops Room was based somewhere near Whiston Grange near Rotherham. Wherever it was situated, the room was described in July 1945 as being essential to the safety and protection of Sheffield. The installation was described as follows:

Safe underground and brilliantly lit with conditioning plants to ensure that the air was kept as fresh as possible. These plants can also filter out gas, although personal gas masks were ready should the need arise. The control room was staffed by

The Old Town Hall, under which there may have been a secret war room.

telephonists whose role would be to take messages and pass them on to service depots. Although there were long hours of duty, the staff were free to play board games, undertake knitting or sewing. However, when the alarm was given these men and women would spring into action. In charge of the control room was an officer whose sole responsibility was for the staff, wardens and administrative officers under him. He would be assisted by plotters and chart writers who locate the 'incident' on a map and decide what services shall be required.

Because of the blackout there were many complaints as people tried to manoeuvre their way around the city. As we have seen, as soon as war was declared, the street lights were put out in Sheffield. So there was a sense of relief when the Sheffield Watch Committee sanctioned new lighting to be switched on the city's 25,000 street lamps on Thursday, 21 December 1939. Metal fittings were attached to the lamps that gave 25-watt-strength lighting over the whole of the city. Mr J.F. Colquhoun, the Corporation Lighting Engineer, told the local newspapers that despite the new lamps, the population of Sheffield should not expect any appreciable relief. The new lights were designed simply to 'take the edge off the absolute blackness.' By February 1940 this new 'Starlight' lighting had been installed in most of the streets of the city centre. Although it remained very dim, the positive difference was noted by workers on their way home at night. The new lighting now enabled people to see the outline of pavements and obstacles more easily. It was less visible in the city centre where there were trams and cars but in the quieter streets it was more noticeable.

Nevertheless, flaws in the blackout of the city were noticed. A flight made by an unnamed pilot of the RAF was read out by the chief constable at a meeting of the Emergency Committee on 15 November 1940. The pilot recorded that on 8 October he had made a survey of the city of Sheffield with Mr Mark Firth of the firm of Thomas Firth and John Brown Ltd. He reported that he had found that street lighting was well blacked-out but the railway marshalling yards were brilliantly illuminated in the night sky. As a consequence of this, a nearby munitions factory was clearly visible. A further flight undertaken on 10 October found five vital steel works in the Don Valley clearly visible from the air. In reply, the chief constable was told that the lights in the marshalling yards were exempt from the blackout but they had instructions to dowse the lights as soon as the warning for an air-raid had been given. As for the steel works, they too had instructions to turn out all lights during an air-raid.

It was announced that air-raid sirens were to be tested for the first time during a weekday at 11 am on Thursday, 11 January 1940. It was reported that during this exercise it was expected that hundreds of air-raid wardens and fire-fighters attached to Sheffield firms would go immediately to their posts once the signal was given. The report claimed that many firms in the city were glad to have the opportunity to add some realism to the regularly-held air-raid practices but in fact it was nearly a disaster. A week later it was reported that the sirens simply could not be heard over the sounds of the industrial machines that were busy producing armaments. However, because they had been accompanied by police whistles, workpeople outside the factories were aware that the sirens had been sounded. They shouted out that the sirens had gone off and consequently much later than expected the workers went to the safety of the shelters. In several districts householders claimed they had heard the whistles before the sirens. Councillor R. Colver complained that 'either the sirens are not powerful enough, or there are not enough of them. They should be strengthened or re-sited or increased in number.' He said that during the day it was essential that sirens must be heard over the sounds of industry in order to protect the workforce. As a consequence of this exercise more sirens were added to various factories around the city.

By Christmas of the first year of the war, some families were delighted to hear that their relatives would be home from France for the festivities. The first Sheffield soldiers to return to the city arrived back on the morning of 19 December 1939 after being given ten days' leave. They told a local reporter that they had no complaints so far, the food was good, they were not rationed and their quarters were comfortable. Their only complaint was that they had to put up with 'too much rain'. About twelve men arrived on the 1.30 pm train and were followed half an hour later by several more. Many of them were met at the station by relatives who packed the platforms. A reporter was there to greet them and he interviewed one man, a former Post Office worker who slung his 96lb pack on his back as he spoke. He too complained that the weather had got much colder, but nevertheless he thanked the people of Sheffield for the cigarettes and other articles that had been sent out to the soldiers. After this short and hurried conversation he dashed off, telling the reporter that his wife was waiting for him at home. Another 'Tommy', who looked no more than 20 years of age, said that his platoon was stationed in a French village and the men were sleeping in barns and outhouses.

Another soldier who returned to the city just in time for New Year found that all his friends and relatives were convinced that he had died. The 22-year-old aircraftman Herbert France arrived back in Sheffield on 29 December. Hearing the news of his death, he went straight away to the Ebenezer Wesleyan Reform Chapel to convince the people of the congregation that he was really alive. It seems that there had been an announcement of the death of A/C B. France who had been killed in action. Because he was always known as 'Bert' to the congregation, they naturally assumed it was the man they all knew. He told them that his name in official circles was Herbert, therefore he was listed as A/C H. France. He received a great response from his friends of the chapel who were just delighted to see that he was still alive.

Thanks to the activities of the civil defence services and the Emergency Committee, most people of Sheffield were now ready for war but the greatest upheaval for most families was that of the parents who had sent their children away to safety, knowing that it might be years before they would see them again.

CHAPTER THREE

The Evacuations

Preliminary preparations for the evacuation of mothers and children from the vulnerable areas of Sheffield had been planned well in advance. The Chief Education Officer Mr H.S. Newton's first task was to establish the numbers of mothers and children that would need to be evacuated when hostilities broke out. Those wishing to be evacuated were instructed to notify the head teachers of the seventy-five different schools in the city. In the initial stages it was estimated that the numbers of persons to be evacuated would be well over 60,000. Meanwhile, Mr Newton contacted other counties as to the number of evacuees they could take. The Emergency Committee was informed in April 1939 that reception areas had been found in Leicestershire and Nottinghamshire. In total they could take 60,300 persons if need be and comprised the following areas:

LEICESTERSHIRE
Barrow upon Soar 9,000
Castle Donnington 2,400
Loughborough 9,000
Melton Mowbray 2,800
Melton & Belvoir 5,500
Shepshed 1,500

NOTTINGHAMSHIRE
Basford 13,000
Bingham 4,000
Newark 4,100
Southwell 9,000

When it was becoming more certain that war was inevitable, Mr Newton gave instructions to the teachers as to how the evacuation process would be carried out. He informed them to notify all the parents regarding exactly what the children were allowed to take with them. They were to carry their gas mask, a change of underclothing, night clothes, spare stockings or socks, a toothbrush, towel, comb, handkerchief, soap, face cloth, a knife, fork, spoon, mug, plate, a warm coat and a mackintosh. Mr Newton instructed the parents that the child's name had to be written on all the items and the children would also have to carry one day's supply of food and water. Once the children had collected the items, they were then to report back to the school at the appointed time given to them. Teachers who were travelling with the children had to ensure that each child had an identity label attached to them. These had the name of the child, its date of birth, home address, name of school and the reception area they would travel to written in black capitals. White armbands would be worn by all the adults helping in the evacuation of children with the initials SEC (Sheffield Education Committee) on them. There would be one adult to every ten children. After their train journey and on their arrival at the reception centre, the leader of the group would report to the billeting officer. They would also be responsible for finding the nearest Post Office and telegraphing the names and addresses of the evacuees to the Chief Education Office. The Sheffield school caretakers would then put that information onto the school notice boards, to notify the parents. The leader of each group would also ensure that they got sufficient postcards from the Post Office for each child to send home with their new address.

On 2 September 1939 the plans that had been put into place were finally confirmed as the first batch of children left Sheffield. There is little doubt that many of the parents would have urged their child to write home as soon as possible. A very welcome letter was received by a Sheffield mother just three days later on 5 September 1939, consisting of six pages. The letter, which was reproduced in the *Sheffield Telegraph and Independent* newspaper, was from an unnamed little girl who described the happy time she was having. Her 'uncle' and 'auntie' had made her feel very welcome and she 'was entertained and fêted like a young princess.' At that time she was making preparations to start a new term at the village school. Other letters were received from those taking care of the evacuees, to reassure mothers that their children had settled in well. One was written by Mrs J.F. Smith who was taking care of a boy called Alan Peacock from Petre Street, Sheffield. She wrote the following to his mother:

I want to put your mind absolutely at rest. Alan is as happy as a little sandboy. I have never seen the sign of a tear yet.

He soon made friends with my little girl and boy and is out
playing all day long. He started to write to you yesterday, but
I am sorry to say that he has been too busy to finish the letter.

She enclosed a photograph showing Alan with her own two
children. Mrs Smith concluded by inviting Mrs Peacock to
visit her any time and added 'My heart grieves for you in your
loneliness.' Parents were encouraged to visit their children
and on Saturday, 16 September 1939 a party of twenty-five
parents from St Silas School, Sheffield travelled to a village near
Leicester. There they found the evacuees having the time of
their lives. Mr Fred Stephens of Hodgson Street, Sheffield was
pleased to see his child looking so happy and declared 'It would
be a crime to bring them back to the city.' Instead of rushing to
greet their parents, the children were too busy showing off their
new clothes. As a treat, Mr Stephens told a reporter that he had
taken a small bag of apples for his children. When he got to the
house where they were staying, he gave the 'lady of the house'
the apples; she laughed and showed him into a room at the back
of the house where there was a ton of apples.

Many of the Sheffield children went to Derwent in Derbyshire
(now under the waters of the Ladybower Reservoir). Although
it was a picturesque little village, there had been complaints
from some of the mothers who had accompanied the children
who were more used to city life. One unnamed mother stated
that she had found it to be so dull after dark. A reporter was sent
to speak to these evacuees and the woman's husband disagreed,
telling him that his wife's opinion was 'bunkum'. He said there
was plenty to do 'if you set your mind to it.' He described how
there were walks during the day and at night there was the radio,
books and the pub for entertainment. He told the reporter 'You
can talk, gossip, knit, drink and smoke and when you get fed
up you can go to bed.' So many children were in fact sent to
Derwent that Gloria Hallett wrote in her diary that regular
buses were put on to run from Sheffield every Sunday in order
for parents to visit their children. The buses left at 1.50 pm and
returned at 4.50 pm.

Some 300 girls of the Sheffield High School were sent
to Calver in the Hope Valley of Derbyshire. The girls were

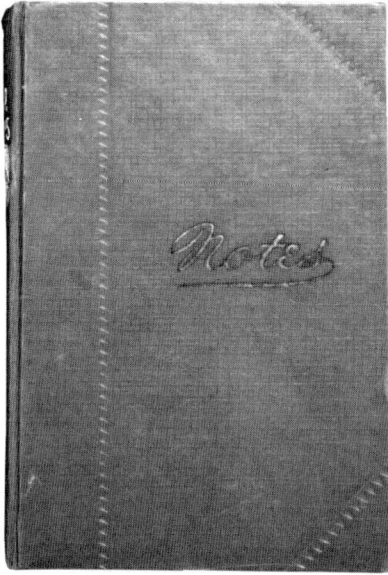

The front of Gloria Hallett's diary.

found accommodation at Cliff College (now a Bible College), a beautiful building surrounded by formal gardens. It was reported at the beginning of February 1940 that the girls had settled in well and brought a sense of excitement to the formerly quiet little village. Their brown uniforms were a familiar sight in the area as they went to and from the college on weekdays under the tutelage of Miss Margaret McCauley, the headmistress. Around eighty of the girls had been billeted out with families in the area but they were invited to entertainments laid on at the college in the evenings. Two of the college pianos had been supplemented by two more from Sheffield as music played a large part in the curriculum. The girls were allowed to listen to the radio and the older girls were allowed to listen to the 6 o'clock news. One of the pupils was the granddaughter of the mayor of Sheffield and two others were the daughters of Sheffield photographer Mr T. Alec Seed who gave weekly photographic evenings at the college.

Beyond urging parents to have their children evacuated, there was little else that the education authorities could do as they simply had no power to enforce evacuation. The scheme had been so successful that in the early months of the war it was estimated that there were fewer than 20,000 children left in the city. However, the authorities feared that the first Christmas of the war would see parents bringing back many of the evacuated children to be with their families. Therefore it was decided that Christmas activities in Sheffield would be kept to a minimum, while evacuated children would be the recipients of lots of parties and games in their new billets. It was reported that for the children still in the city 'It is probable that they would have the dullest Christmas on record, as all Christmas parties were banned.'

On the outbreak of war most Sheffield schools had been closed but by 15 September 1939 the Sheffield Education Committee was considering what to do with the children that remained in the city who still required their education. They decided to establish an Education at Home scheme that had never been tried before. The Education Officer Mr Newton and his deputy Dr W.P. Alexander announced plans for the scheme which, with the permission of parents, would involve teachers visiting the children's homes. As time went on, several children

Excerpt from Gloria Hallett's diary saying that Mrs Trotter 'had 12 King Edward Grammar School boys coming every day…'

would gather together in larger rooms and the teacher would visit on appointed days of the week. One of the advantages of the scheme was that teachers would be able to teach smaller groups of children instead of large classes of thirty to forty pupils. Head teachers would remain responsible for the maintenance of the 'home service' and would allocate sections to each member of staff. The plan relied on the co-operation of individual parents facilitating space in their homes to undertake such work. In Gloria Hallett's diary she describes a woman called Mrs Trotter who had '12 King Edward Grammar School boys coming every day for a week under the Government scheme for continuing education for children not evacuated.' She also mentions another woman, 'Miss Easton's sister', who made 'quite a nice little schoolroom in an upper room which I am lending her for emergency classes.'

For those schools that did remain open there was still the risk of bombing and following the blitz in December 1940 several schools had been hit. In January 1941, Mr Alexander announced to the Education Committee that the Maud Maxfield School for the Deaf had been totally demolished and the College of Arts and Crafts had been so badly damaged that it was going to be difficult to reopen. A part of the new Abbeydale Grammar School had suffered a direct hit in the north-east corner, which had left a shortage of school places. The only solution was to arrange for the children to have half-time education in shifts. One group would be in school from 9 am to noon and another group would be in school from 1 pm to 4 pm.

By June of 1940 the war situation was so serious that many parents were being encouraged to register their older children for overseas evacuation to the Dominions. It was reported on 27 June that many mothers were leaving their prams outside the Sheffield Education Office in order to go inside to register their children's names. Some mothers were offering to go with their children aged between 5 and 16 on board ship and to look after them when they reached their destination. However, for many women the choice between keeping the children at home or sending them away was a terrible one. As one Sheffield mother told a reporter: 'I can't make my mind up. I only have one girl and I just don't know what to do for the best.' So many offers to look after the children were coming in from parents in Canada, Australia and the United States that organizations were taking on the responsibility of transporting the children safely to their destination. Others would be sent out to friends or relatives of their parents. One of the first to go was Margaret Foster, the 11-year-old daughter of Reverend J.E. Foster, the vicar of St Michael's, Neepsend, Sheffield. She had been attending Oakwood Collegiate School, Sheffield before going to St Hilda's Church of England boarding school at Whitby. It was announced on 3 July that all the girls from the school under the age of 16 would be going to Canada. When Margaret finally returned home in February of 1945, Reverend Foster told a reporter that she was 'quite grown up now.' He had been given leave from where he was stationed as chaplain in Holland to meet her. They spent a memorable leave chatting happily about events that had taken place since they had been separated. Margaret told him that she had been kindly treated in Canada and made lots of friends while she was there.

Two other evacuees who also went to Canada were 15-year-old Audrey Crookes and her sister Avril aged 12. They sent a letter to their parents at Ecclesall Road South, Sheffield that was printed in the *Sheffield Telegraph and Independent* of 3 September 1940. The girls stated that the first part of the letter had been written in the parlour car of a train on its way to Toronto. On board the train the girls had been served with apple juice, lamb chops, potatoes and cabbage in butter, ice cream and fruit cake, a menu that must have made their parents mouths' water in heavily-rationed Sheffield. The two sisters then travelled to Hamilton where they were staying with a friend of the family, Mrs Douglas Hobson. They described how the weather was so hot that most Canadian children wore only their bathing costumes for much of the day. Audrey and Avril described leaving their parents and the moment when the ship set sail from a British port. The letter said how both girls were seasick in the choppy water that developed a day or so out to sea. Audrey said that it gradually got worse and she didn't eat much. In order to combat the seasickness she tried walking around the decks and as a consequence had lost 3in off her waist. The letter concluded: 'This house is very lovely, but I haven't time to describe it now as we are just going swimming at a friend's pool and I want to post this. I will draw some pictures of the rooms and send them to you soon.'

Four years later Audrey arrived back in Sheffield where she too looked so grown-up that her parents barely recognized her. She told them that she had enjoyed her time in Canada and her sister had so enjoyed it that it was unclear whether or not she would return to Sheffield. For the first three years they had attended Strathallen, a well-known girls' school in Hamilton. It was reported that she spoke with a Canadian accent as she told her parents she had won a scholarship for the Slade School of Art in London.

Six Sheffield children were evacuated to South Africa on 18 August 1940, arriving at Cape Town a month later. They were Ronnie, Earnest and Barbara Stevenson of Wisewood Avenue, Shirley and Audrey Robinson of Struan Road, and Audrey Furniss of Peel Street, Broomhill. The children's ages ranged from 11 to 14 and on the journey they were kept busy with physical training, games and celebrating birthday parties as well as school, church, medical parades and lessons in Afrikaans. At the final meal on board ship the children each found a shilling that had been placed under their plates by the stewards who had waited on them during the voyage. They also told their parents that once land was in sight they cheered themselves up by singing patriotic songs such as *There'll Always be an England*. The Cape Town newspapers also reported the children's arrival, stating that 'Men and women, who met the children at the docks, confessed afterwards that it was a thrilling moment as the ship docked with its cheering cargo.' In their next letter the two sisters Shirley and Audrey Robinson described their arrival in a letter dated 21 September. As they walked around Cape Town, most South Africans seemed to know who they were as they shouted out 'welcome' to the two girls.

Another Sheffield evacuee was 12-year-old Geoffrey William Stevens who, on the way to Australia, docked at South Africa where he spent the day with a 19-year-old girl named Enid Boyce. After Geoffrey had gone on the next part of his journey, Enid took the chance to write to his parents at Southey Hall Drive, Sheffield in October of 1940. She wrote that Geoffrey had left South Africa with nine other children and she too described the welcome they had been given by the people of Cape Town. She told his parents: 'Last night when it was time for him to go aboard for the last leg of his journey, it was like parting with my own brother. I really enjoyed the day in his company and I can say that he thoroughly enjoyed himself too.' She told them that the children had each been given a book signed by 'our Mayor' Mr Smitts and he then got the Lady Mayoress to sign it too. A few weeks later Geoffrey himself wrote to his parents to let them know that he had landed safely in Australia and he reported the conditions on board ship. Heading his letter 'Somewhere on the ocean wave, the world', he wrote

> This is a grand ship, there is a swimming pool, a games room and last night we had a concert and tonight a film show. Today we had the Crossing the Line Ceremony and it was funny. Sailors with just trunks and head gear turned the hosepipes on us and then chased us.

It was reported that Geoffrey was heading for Perth where a female friend of Mr and Mrs Stevens, who had been the daughter of a former Sheffield man, was about to take charge of him.

Parents who had sent their children away to other countries must have breathed a sigh of relief when they arrived safely. So many ships were the targets of raiders, whether they carried evacuated children or not. One Sheffield woman, Mrs Connie Fox, had been married for just three weeks before the ship on which she was travelling was torpedoed. Thankfully the vessel was returning from escorting some evacuee children to Australia from Sheffield and consequently just the adults were on board. The ship had been one of the first to take Sheffield evacuees to Australia in November 1940. Nearly three years later in June 1943 the *Sheffield Telegraph* printed an account of her journey. The ship was shelled by Germans in between Adelaide and Durban. Five shells hit the ship and one, which failed to explode, went through the bathroom where Connie would normally have been in the bath. The ship that had hit them thankfully took on board the survivors, although they were not allowed to take any luggage with them. They watched from the deck of the enemy vessel as their ship blazed up to the sky before sinking. The party was then transferred to a captured Norwegian tanker and Mrs Fox became one of 500 prisoners, only nine of which were women. She finally reached the only female internee camp in Germany, arriving there in April 1941. She described the camp which was filled with women and children and said there were about eleven different languages to be heard. A decision was made to find a common language and English classes were soon being taught. In the confusion of the packed internee camp, Mrs Fox started a Wolf Cub and Brownie pack for the children. She told a reporter from the *Sheffield Telegraph* that gradually the food provided in the camp got worse. Breakfast was usually a piece of bread, jam and coffee, and dinner was soup with a second course of a pudding or a vegetable. Only occasionally were the prisoners ever given meat. Supper consisted of bread and coffee or cocoa to drink. They were only kept alive by the Red Cross food parcels that they received regularly. She was finally repatriated from Palestine in October 1942. Safely back with her sister-in-law, Mrs Henry Dixon of Mylnhurst Road, Eccleshall, Sheffield, Mrs Fox told the reporter that she was delighted to be reunited with her husband, Captain Reverend G.S. Fox, a chaplain in the army. When she originally left Sheffield to accompany the children, she had no idea that their separation would last three years.

One of the organizations that evacuated British children to the United States was the employers of men and women of the Warner Brothers Film Company. Almost as soon as war broke out, the company offered to take evacuated children. One of those who took advantage of this offer was a Mr Nelson, the South Yorkshire representative of the company. He sent his 15-year-old stepdaughter Jean Mary Wood and 12-year-old son Anthony John Nelson over to Long Island, New York. At Christmas 1940 the BBC informed Mrs Nelson of Norton Lane, Sheffield that her 15-year-old daughter would have a message for her the following day. The broadcast included messages from several other Sheffield children and would have been particularly poignant. Mrs Nelson told a reporter after the broadcast that 'it was as if her daughter Jean was talking to us from the same room. It was so marvellously clear.' Jean told her mother that 'she wished her brothers, sisters and the budgerigar a happy Christmas and the hope that we are all safe.'

By October 1940 there had been little bombing in Sheffield and so it was decided that the city would play host to some of the mothers and children from the south of Britain. On 22 October 1940 there were plenty of helpers from the WVS (Women's Voluntary Services), the ARP and other emergency feeding organizations to meet the evacuees arriving at the LMS (London, Midland and Scottish) station in Sheffield. Most of the passengers had no idea where Sheffield was prior to their arrival and many appeared to be weary and anxious from lack of sleep following the heavy bombing in and around the capital. Some of them had already been moved out of the heavily-bombed dockland areas of London and had sad stories to tell to the helpers who greeted them with much-needed cups of tea and biscuits and bags of sweets for the children. The women and children were split up into several groups: some went to the City General Hospital; others to the Fir Vale Centre, Wharncliffe Hospital and Nether Edge Hospital. The groups were then transported to the different centres and their luggage sorted by groups of volunteers to make sure that it went to the right place. By this time the treatment of evacuees had been well-practised and those of them that were sent to the Fir Vale Centre were greeted with a hot meal of hotpot and bread, followed by tinned fruit and custard. The younger children were given milk and biscuits. When the meal was over, arrangements had been made for everyone to have a bath before retiring to bed for a well-earned sleep. Little children slept in bunks next to their mothers, while boys and girls over the age of 10 had dormitories of their own. Staff had been instructed to ensure that the families had a day of 'ease and comfort', starting the following morning with a cup of tea in bed. This was soon followed by a sausage breakfast at 9.30 am. Dinner consisted of fried fish and chips, roast apples, rice pudding, tea and milk, and breakfast sausages were served for their tea. Everyone was issued with a banana, an apple and an orange. During their stay, many spoke about the bombings that took place night after night and the cold hard underground station stones that had been their beds during these raids. They told of the comforting roar of the anti-aircraft guns firing at enemy planes during the raids. They described how, when they emerged from the underground station, they found damaged streets, wrecked homes and lost friends. Many of them spoke about their husbands having to go to work for weeks on end without a proper night's sleep.

A reporter was sent to interview some of the evacuees and found them listening to a singing concert at the Fir Vale Centre. One little girl, who only a few hours previously had been sheltering from a raid in London, sang a song. Her mother was in the audience, as were other mothers, some still wearing

Excerpt from Gloria Hallett's diary: '... given cocoa for his supper, asked "What the hell's this?"'

bandages where they had been cut by flying glass. The women joined in with the singing and proceeded to sing other songs. These were love songs, sea shanties and patriotic songs all designed to cheer the families who were miles away from their homes. One 60-year-old woman told the reporter 'We would rather die than live under Hitler.' The following day the mothers and children were allotted billets in other towns, cities and villages over the West Riding of Yorkshire. Nevertheless, there were some strange stories circulating in Sheffield about these weird evacuees from towns in the south. Gloria Hallett in her diary relates how one boy, when given cocoa for his supper, asked his anxious host 'What the hell's this?' His sister explained and told him to 'drink it up', to which he replied 'But I always have beer for my supper.'

Despite the warmth of the welcome, only a few weeks later in November 1940 it was reported that out of the sixty-eight mothers and children evacuated to the moorland village of Stannington, Sheffield, most of them had returned to London. They had spent all their lives in a big city and found that rural life did not suit them at all. Some stated that separation from husbands and fathers had proved too much of a trial and they had decided to return home and share the risks. Speaking to a reporter, one of the inhabitants stated that when it became known that some of the mothers had decided to return, other mothers quickly joined them. Others allowed themselves no time to settle in and returned home after just a couple of good nights' sleep. In one case a husband arrived to take his wife and child back with him, saying that he could not bear to be parted from them. However, it was reported that these few were the exception and that many of the other mothers and children had settled in well at Stannington. The village, which is set in rolling hills where the vista is peaceful and full of farm animals, played host to other mothers who happily sent their children to the local council school. The reporter stated that in the playground there was a mixture of broad Yorkshire and cockney accents.

Throughout the war it must have been very difficult for parents dreadfully missing their children who were hundreds of miles away. So it was perhaps the best news of all after the war was over on 3 May 1945 that the first train carrying the evacuated mothers and children home from Sheffield would arrive in a few days' time. Parents were informed that they would soon receive, from the local authority in which they were living, a notice telling them of the return home plans. Within a week a census was to be taken to find out exactly how many evacuees had already returned home. Mr Henry Willink MP, Minister of Health, said thank you on behalf of the government to all those householders who had sheltered evacuees in Sheffield since the beginning of the war.

CHAPTER FOUR

The Sheffield Home Guard

L ong before the outbreak of war, in 1936 the government was looking for the best way of defending each individual town and city by using local men who knew their own area. Before the concept of the Home Guard was born, the War Office established the National Defence Company. They issued an invitation to join this scheme to all ex-soldiers and more than 3,000 from the Sheffield and district area volunteered. On 24 August 1939, ten days before war was declared, these men were mobilized and posted to guarding the more vital areas of the city such as petrol and military stores, aerodromes and rail and river bridges. The scheme worked successfully for a time; however, by May of 1940 matters were becoming more serious and there was a real risk of invasion by enemy forces. The government wanted a body of men who could, in case of invasion, slow the enemy down until regular soldiers could take charge of the situation. It had been agreed that such a force would have to be composed of those too old or too young to enlist in the armed services, or those in reserved occupations. It was also established that the new force would be called the Local Defence Volunteers (LDV), and they would be recruited through the many police stations in the towns and cities of Britain.

It was said that within minutes of the historic speech made by Anthony Eden on 14 May 1940 asking for men to join the LDV, the first man from Sheffield was already handing in his name at the police station. Eden had told his listening public: 'We want large numbers of men in Great Britain who are British subjects between the ages of 17 and 65 to come forward now and offer their services in order to make assurance [that an invasion would be repelled] double sure.'

So anxious were these men to enlist and play a part in the defence of Britain that many police officers had not yet been informed of the scheme by their superiors. For the next few hours there was a steady stream of Sheffield volunteers and the local authorities were totally unprepared for the numbers of persons that did respond. Within a matter of days the War Office appointed Colonel F.A. Neill to head more than 300 men from Sheffield and district and turn them into an integrated unit. It was a daunting task indeed. The immediate problem facing him was how to train so many volunteers and how to arm them and provide them all with uniforms. Many of those that volunteered in these early days were students at Sheffield University. It had been agreed by the government that they would continue to study while carrying out their duties for the LDV. The rest were made up of men who would continue with their usual daily work and undertake patrols and drills at nights and weekends.

Colonel Neill organized his headquarters to be at his place of work at Napier Street and he soon appointed Colonel D.S. Branson to be his assistant commander. The LDV would use the same five sections of the city that the police were already using and sectional commanders were appointed to take responsibility for each of these divisions. Within seventy-two hours the Sheffield LDV was operational. They took over the duties of the National Defence Company, protecting vulnerable areas and holding regular patrols from dusk to dawn, even though at that point many of the men had no uniforms. Ten days later, a staff conference had been arranged with all the local civil defence services to decide how best to defend the city. Physical training was the order of the day and men were trained at drill halls, parks and playing fields around the city. Despite the quick response to enlist in the LDV, the service soon became the butt of jokes and ridicule that would dog it throughout the war and

Colonel F.A. Neill, commander of the Sheffield Home Guard.

Some Home Guard members without uniforms.

beyond. It hardly helped that initially the men had no weapons apart from sticks or broom handles, and as a result of this the men were known as the 'broomstick army' for a while. They still had no uniforms; just an armband with LDV embroidered on it. Only when the men became known as the 'Look, Duck and Vanish' brigade was the name changed to the Home Guard in July 1940.

All weapons had been handed into the military authorities at the outbreak of war and Colonel Neill had to get his men armed as quickly as possible. Some weapons were donated, such as eighty Lee Enfield rifles from the Senior Training Corps at the university. Gradually the men who would form the Sheffield Home Guard became an organized and professional deterrent. Colonel Neill encouraged the different groups across the city to develop a close communication with the other civil defence groups as well as local regular troops. Almost immediately the Home Guard was given sentry duty at the open-air parts of the city, such as golf courses and parks where it was thought that enemy paratroopers might land. It was also decided that signposts would be removed around Sheffield in order to cause confusion to any enemy troops that might invade. By Sunday, 25 August 1940 the Sheffield Home Guard was confident enough to join in a three-hour demonstration with other civil defence groups in front of 5,000 spectators. It was reported that the men took their role very seriously and showed tremendous enthusiasm: 'The men taking expert instruction in mounting guard gave a demonstration of bayoneting practice with all appropriate belligerence and aggressive gestures. Bren guns were manned with speed and were fired in the prone, kneeling and upright positions.'

In addition the City Engineers gave a demonstration of cleaning up a road covered in mustard gas and ARP wardens showed how to put out incendiary bombs with a stirrup pump. First-aid parties also dealt with mock casualties and the AFS gave a convincing display of fire-fighting. It was reported that 'at last the womenfolk could see that the men engaged in civil defence didn't spend their time making tea or exchanging yarns.'

Colonel Neill had made such progress in turning the Sheffield Home Guard into a professional group of part-time soldiers that when the men were on parade in September for Lieutenant General Sir Ronald Adams, he was impressed by the smart turn-out. The commander-in-chief, after inspecting the men, told a reporter that 'The fine thing about the Sheffield Home Guard was the mixture of old and young soldiers, which was just what they wanted.' In the course of his inspection Lieutenant General Adam stopped to talk to several old soldiers and asked them questions about their medals. The Lord Mayor, Alderman J.A. Longden, who accompanied the general, said that 'It was the most inspiring event of my year of office. More parades should be held to arouse the admiration of the public and show them what is being done for their protection.'

One legless ex-serviceman summed up the general feeling the public had for their own Home Guard. He told a reporter 'They are a credit to Sheffield.' Following the inspection, Lieutenant General Adam and the Lord Mayor took their place at the Town Hall while crowds of people cheered as the men paraded smartly past. Headed by mounted police and the

Lieut General Sir R. Adams inspects the men.

Sheffield Police band, the men presented an inspiring spectacle. Veterans of the previous world war marched proudly at the side of younger men, while the motorized section was reported to be 'most impressive'. However, the men of the Sheffield Home Guard showed their true mettle following the heavy bombing on the nights of the blitz. The men turned out in force to help the rescue services, to searches for casualties caught in the bombing, they evacuated people from the most dangerous areas to rest centres and assisted in patrol duties. Following the bombing, Councillor Asbury in his position as chair of the Emergency Committee paid great tribute not only to the Home Guard but also the civil defence men and women who served the area with 'great bravery and complete unselfishness over the past few days'. He said 'the bravery and courage of the services can only be compared with that of soldiers in the field of battle.'

Throughout the war years the Sheffield Home Guard held several regular exercises, which were designed to co-ordinate with the other defence services. On Sunday, 26 October 1941 it was agreed that it would be designated 'the Battle of Sheffield day' as an invasion exercise. The local newspaper reported that 'it was going to be one of the biggest and most comprehensive exercises undertaken so far, when tear gas and thunder flashes will be used.' It was arranged that the attacking forces would be the regular troops disguised as 'fifth columnists' that would begin sabotage operations across the city at an unspecified hour. They would then be followed by enemy airborne troops who would fight their way into the city centre, destroying vital points. Exactly how the attack was to be carried out was kept a closely-guarded secret. Civilians were asked through the local newspapers to 'stay put' at home, and on no account were they to hamper the operation or take part in any of the 'fighting'. They were warned that the exercise was 'not a matter for jollification, but a serious exercise to test the efficiency of the civil defence services.'

The imaginary sequence of events to unfold would begin with the supposed capture of a German officer from a crashed reconnaissance plane that had come down on the east coast. Papers were to be found on him that would reveal the intended airborne attack 'in or near Sheffield', along with instructions as to the elimination of vital targets in the area. A reporter stated that during the 'battle' it was interesting to note how well the combined efforts of the military, police and civil defence organizations worked closely together, despite a few communication problems. In order to combat these difficulties, messages were sent via runners on motorcycles and bicycles who knew the area and in particular how to use back streets away from the fighting. One Home Guard unit made great use of a rigged-up lamp signal for sending messages that could only be read by a recipient standing in an exact position. The police authorities improvised their own communications through the use of a car that had been adapted to receive wireless messages. This gave good service until it was 'captured' by enemy forces. However, at the end of the day the exercise was a failure as the 'enemy' bombers and parachutists took the very vital targets that were supposed to be defended. The result was the taking of the railway station and the 'destruction' of a gas holder.

Nevertheless, despite the fact that there were over eighty major incidents, no effort had been spared to make the whole 'battle' as realistic as possible. One particular incident took place at the junction of Attercliffe Road and Effingham Street, where it was suggested that a high-explosive bomb had fallen. Dummies had been placed under wreckage as substitutes for real bodies and many tons of earth thrown across the road. It was also supposed that the area was contaminated with mustard gas and as a result the traffic between Sheffield, Rotherham and Tinsley was held up. Tramcars were stopped and passengers had to be ferried across the city using buses. Men in large mechanical diggers were brought in to remove the debris and a decontamination squad was brought in to clear the air. Rescue squads went through the rubble looking for bodies, and fire crews dealt expertly with the many fires that broke out. Virtually every service was brought in to play their part and, despite the outcome, it was generally agreed that the Sheffield Home Guard as well as the other services had acquitted themselves very well indeed.

It was often jokingly said that many of the men of the Home Guard were four times more likely to die in an accident during training than in carrying out their duties and this was sadly proved correct in an accident that occurred in September 1941.

An inquest was held by Sheffield City Coroner Mr J. Kenyon Parker on the deceased body of a man. He was 52-year-old James Lionel Fleming of Lydgate Hall Crescent who had been shot at the Home Guard post when a live bullet had been left in a rifle that was thought to be empty. A Home Guard volunteer, Eric Ashmore of Western Road, Sheffield gave evidence that he heard that an alarm had been raised at 1.30 am on 4 September 1941. He went with Home Guard Sergeant Burden to investigate and when he returned, the sergeant took his rifle before giving him his own, which he said was empty. Sergeant Joseph Thomas Burden of Springfield Road, Sheffield gave evidence that after taking Ashmore's rifle he discharged what he thought was the one bullet remaining in it. As he held it 'at port' (held diagonally in front of the body, with the muzzle pointing upwards), the trigger was accidentally pulled. To his complete amazement the gun went off and fired into the ceiling. Later it was found that upstairs Fleming was lying in bed and had received a bullet wound to his knee. He died in hospital following an operation to have his leg amputated.

Sergeant Burden stated that prior to that evening when men were handed ammunition it was given to them as individual bullets, but on this occasion a clip with five cartridges in it had been issued. Therefore when he discharged the one bullet from Ashmore's gun, he assumed that it was then empty. Mr F.W. Scorah who attended the inquest on behalf of the Home Guard Service expressed his very great sympathy for Fleming's relatives. He told the inquest that the training for the men in the use of rifles was very thorough and although thousands of men had been trained, this was the first such incident in the city. The jury returned a verdict that Fleming died from a gunshot wound due to the negligent discharge of a live cartridge. They concluded that they did not consider this to be of a criminal nature but added that more care should have been taken in the issue of ammunition. Mr Kenyon Parker said that he concurred with their decision, but added that 'It was an accident which should not have happened.'

In 1942 it was thought by the War Office that the anti-aircraft units of large towns and cities should be taken over by the Home Guard, leaving the regular soldiers who had previously fired them

The men of the Anti-Aircraft Battery.

to take their places in the offensive forces. Therefore in April 1942 Colonel Neill was requested to form such a unit from the Sheffield Home Guard that was initially called a 'Z' Battery, before being changed to the 101 Anti-Aircraft Battery. Rotherham was also to have its own anti-aircraft unit and so in June 1942 recruitment for men from Sheffield and Rotherham was held at Porter Street, Sheffield and Wellgate, Rotherham. Recruitment was strong in Sheffield from people who wanted not only to take a real part in the defence of the city, but also a way to get back at the enemy in revenge for the horrors of the blitz. By the end of July 1942 the Sheffield section (101 Battery) was fully manned with two guns based at Shirecliffe and Manor. A third gun was based at Brinsworth, near Rotherham. Many of the men who were volunteering for the unit had been gunners in the last war. However, they found the rocket guns very strange weapons compared to those they had previously known. In addition to their ordinary training, the men were now trained in the use of anti-aircraft guns and rocket-launchers at the coastal town of Mablethorpe at the weekends, where they were able to fire the rockets across the water. They proudly wore a badge of a red flash with bow and arrow markings as they fought alongside their regular army comrades. At the beginning of December 1943 a better practice site was found on the moors at Midhope. This was ideally situated as it had acres of moorland around it, although warning had to be given in advance to farmers and gamekeepers of the area.

There had been some problems with employers who were reluctant to allow some of their workers who served in the Home Guard to have time off for training and in September of that year Colonel Neill was castigating them. Through the columns of the local newspaper, these employers were urged to release members of the units in order to undertake training that was vital for the defence of the city. There were also problems for the men asking their employers for week-long training at camps away from home. They were requested to ensure that such volunteers did not suffer from any significant loss of pay during such training. Colonel Neill

Rocket guns which the Home Guard learned to fire.

told them that the chief problem was that employers could do a great deal more to help the unit than they had thus far. Colonel Neill stated that the excuse from the employers was always the same – that the need to keep up production was paramount – but as he pointed out, 'All the production in the world would mean nothing if this country was invaded.' He said that the Sheffield Home Guard was now better trained and better armed than it had been two years previously, and their ranks had been joined by several specialist instructors, regular army officers and warrant officers. He concluded that to achieve this, training was essential and that 'Invasion of this country will bring a grim battle against a ruthless enemy, in which no quarter will be given or expected by us. It is not our army, it is **your** army. It is therefore your duty to help the Home Guard to defend this city.'

Because of the intense training and lack of places to practise, it was not until May 1943 that the first guns were fully manned by Home Guard personnel. Right from the first announcement that the Sheffield Home Guard would take over the anti-aircraft units, the military authorities had been sceptical. They doubted that it was possible to train the men in their spare time to a sufficiently high standard to have any effect on the enemy planes. In fact, their performance exceeded all expectations. In March 1944 Colonel Neill made arrangements for the Sheffield and Rotherham anti-aircraft men of the Home Guard to spend their weekends in London. This was for a dual purpose: to man the sites, therefore giving them more experience of firing; and to relieve the hard-pressed London Home Guard, giving them a well-earned rest from the heavy bombing they were experiencing. The men were sent to batteries in Southwark, Battersea and Hyde Park and were so popular that when the weekend trips were stopped due to transport restrictions prior to the D-Day landings, there was almost a riot.

By the time the Sheffield Home Guard held another two-day invasion exercise in January 1943, it was generally agreed that considerable improvements had been made in the way they had carried out their duties. Once again teams from the police force, the fire service and the civil defence teams took part. Comparisons were inevitably made between this and the last big exercise in October 1941, when the defending forces had been roundly trounced. One of the *Sheffield Telegraph* reporters described it:

Today the city of Sheffield resembled a gigantic pin-table. Over the whole area there has been established a close network of defended localities, the object of which is to deny the enemy the use of roads and other means of communication. I saw some of them yesterday. The Home Guard were so excellently camouflaged as to be invisible until one was on top of them. The 'enemy forces' were also equipped with good, heavy, high powered weapons, and as a result the civil defence services were severely tested by them. The NFS, whilst dealing with smaller fires and cut off from reinforcements, were suddenly called upon to concentrate with much larger outbreaks. Civil defence workers, already stretched in dealing with their own outbreaks, also had prisoners thrust into their charge.

Both organizers of the exercise, Lieutenant General T.R. Eastwood (Northern Command) and Major General Sir

A disguised Home Guard sniper.

William Bartholomew (Regional Commissioner), concluded that the operation had been a great success. They spoke of the great enthusiasm experienced from both sides, and in particular those snipers who were virtually invisible. However, they still felt that more work needed to be done, and better lines of communication between the services developed.

For many years the wives, mothers, sisters and sweethearts of the men of the Sheffield Home Guard had also volunteered to help out at the headquarters. In December 1941 they unofficially formed themselves into the Women's Home Defence Corps. Like their menfolk, they often worked during the day at their full-time jobs and would volunteer in the evening to help with any non-combatant jobs. Consequently they undertook such tasks as sorting rations, doing first-aid, helping with clerical work or making camouflage nets. These women and girls were so keen to join the Corps that they even used their valuable clothing coupons to have a kind of uniform made. This consisted of khaki shirts, brown skirts and dark-coloured berets. By March 1943 these women amounted to almost 200 and they had their own commandant, the wife of the Home Guard Commandant Lieutenant Colonel A.F. Mackenzie. She appointed women into the positions of first leader and second leader, wearing armbands to indicate their status. Mrs Mackenzie told a reporter that she was very proud of her Corps and said that 'many of them are so keen that they come in nearly every night, giving every spare moment to it.'

The Corps was visited the following month by Dr Edith Summerskill, herself a staunch champion of the Women's Home Defence movement that she had started in December 1941. She praised the women of Sheffield for the work they had done and said how much the government appreciated their role. Not only had they taken part in cooking and driving, but in latter years had been involved in intelligence, signalling and communications. She later told a reporter that all the women had to take a six-week training course in musketry, although they were clearly not under military discipline. The question of uniform was a matter entirely for the volunteers to decide for themselves. Although they had to be approved by the commandant before 'going on the strength', they could resign at any time. Lieutenant Colonel Mackenzie also added his praise for the Corps, and particularly for those women who had been volunteering right from the formation of the LDV.

In April 1943 the Sheffield Home Guard had an invitation to go to London on Saturday, 3 April to witness a street-fighting demonstration. The invitation had been extended by Lord

Officers and men of the Home Guard in London, March 1943.

Kemsley himself, who had conceived the idea of a home defence force well before the formation of the LDV had been announced. The men were met by his son, the Honourable Lionel Berry, and Major Reginald Simpson, the commanding officer of C Company, 5 Battalion, City of London Home Guard. Major Simpson paid tribute to Colonel Neill and conveyed cordial greetings to the men from Sheffield. Colonel Neill returned his thanks and stated that the Home Guard had been called upon to play many roles and might have new ones before them. Nevertheless, they were all united 'to do what they could for their country.' The men then watched the demonstration by the London Home Guard who had evolved their own technique of street-fighting, using different operations. Some advanced along a road held by the enemy by climbing the sides of houses and making themselves practically invisible. One observer noted that for as long as three minutes the men showed remarkable self-control by 'freezing' and remaining completely motionless. Using simple camouflage, these armed men completely merged into the background and were not spotted by the 'enemy' dressed in Gestapo uniforms. The demonstration was topped off when the London Home Guard made a successful 'raid' on 'Gestapo Headquarters' using blanks and fireworks. Then the day was rounded off by the company's fife and drum band, which it was reported had already won fame in the City of London. Colonel Neill chatted with members of the band and offered the whole company his warm congratulations on their splendid show, which he said 'had certainly given my own men and myself a lot to think about.'

On 16 May 1943 the third anniversary of the Sheffield Home Guard was held with an impressive Home Guard Sunday Parade through the streets of the city. In spite of transport strikes, thousands of people gathered to watch this parade of local men. Once described by Major John Hay Beith, the Director of Public Relations at the War Office, as an 'improvised, unarmed and slightly bewildered last hope, they were now a disciplined and properly armed branch of His Majesty's forces.' The people of Sheffield cheered the long ranks of men and the centre of the city was thronged with spectators as the men were inspected by Colonel W. Howson, the commanding officer. The company assembled at Barker's Pool at 11 am to find their band playing regimental marches. Transport vehicles lined Holly Street and Balm Green, loaded with military weapons on display to the public. Following a service at the cathedral, a march past was held in Castle Street before Colonel Mark Firth, the AA brigade commander. The day continued with another parade in Millhouses Park that concluded with a drumhead service led by Reverend H. McIntyre, followed by a display by a motorcyclist company. Special interest was shown in the khaki-clad members of the Women's Home Defence Corps at the Owlerton Sports Stadium in the afternoon, where Mrs Mackenzie witnessed

Home Guard inspection in May 1943.

her troops holding demonstrations of communications using semaphore and carrier pigeons.

In November 1943 one of the Sheffield Home Guard was selected to be drawn in pastels by the British artist Eric Kennington. He was undertaking the commission for a new book on the Home Guard, which was to be written by John Brophy, the author of more than forty books. The chosen man was 52-year-old Harry Dawson, a production manager at James Neill and Co. He was a battery sergeant in the Home Guard and lived at City Road, Sheffield. He had been chosen as a typical representative of 'a Sheffielder who mans the city anti-aircraft batteries.' In the same month another article on the Sheffield Home Guard was written by war correspondent Alfred Dow who met some more of the men. He emphasized the dedication of the Home Guard and wrote about one young furnace man who worked eleven hours a day, six days a week and still turned out for his duties on three nights during the week and once on Sundays. Dow also listed other men whose ages ranged from 17 to 45, all of whom were employed in strenuous manual jobs and working long hours, yet they still had a great enthusiasm for the parades. Dow met Second Lieutenant S. Powell of Leigh Street, Sheffield who had joined as a volunteer in November 1942. He worked a night shift of seventy-two hours a week at Brown Bayleys Steelworks as a furnace man. Because Powell worked nights, he was told that he might not qualify for anti-aircraft duties. He protested so vigorously against this that they finally allowed him to be on duty every Saturday evening after finishing his own work until 5 am the next day. Another man gave his name as Lance Corporal V. Siddall of Hurlfield Avenue, Sheffield. He told Dow that in the last war he had served with the Hallamshire Regiment and his son was serving with them at that time as a CSM. He also told Dow that he was proud 'to be on active service again.'

A section of some of the men of the anti-aircraft battalion left Sheffield in June 1944 to play a vital part in the defence of the City of London and the south from the German V-weapon attacks. Consequently it was not until 13 July that this particular brigade was finally disbanded. Their Brigadier Major B. Chichester Cooke, who was awarded a CBE, paid tribute not only to the men of the Home Guard but also the Sheffield

Corporation employees with whom he had worked closely. He stated to a reporter that:

> I like to think that in Sheffield the relations between the air defences and the Corporation were an example to the whole country. The officials of the city supported and helped me in everything however inconvenient. The Lord Mayor [then Councillor S.H. Marshall] never refused me his active assistance. The City Treasurer [Mr A.B. Griffiths], the City Engineer [Mr J.M. Collie] and the Water Engineer [then Mr J.K. Swales] gave me invaluable help, whilst the Town Clerk [Mr J. Heys] threw himself wholeheartedly into our joint problems. I cannot thank them enough.

Major Chichester Cooke told the reporter that he was proud of the men of the battalion from as high as Mr Mark Firth down to the most recently-joined man and said that 'if the enemy had come they would have shown their prowess to the world.' What was not revealed at the time was that during the practice for the Dambusters raid, Major Chichester Cooke and 5,000 members of the Sheffield anti-aircraft battery had played a vital part in the training of the pilots. The unit had moved into the Lakeland part of Sheffield, camping out on the very banks of the water. They took with them guns, searchlights and smoke units in order to defend the area.

As we have seen, the Sheffield Home Guard had proved to be a professional, skilled band of men well able to defend the city of Sheffield, and so it was with some dismay that it was announced that arrangements were in place for them to be 'stood down'. The Emergency Committee was informed on 12 September 1944 that their duty would cease in December. Three days later the committee expressed to the commander Colonel Neill and the officers and men and women of the Sheffield Home Guard their sincere appreciation and admiration:

> of the manner in which they prepared themselves at great personal sacrifice to defend the city in the event of an invasion. The presence of the Home Guard and the high state of preparedness to which the service attained undoubtedly

inspired confidence during the period of peril through which the nation passed, and in no small measure contributed to the grand spirit of defiance which was characteristic at that time.

The ceremony when the Home Guard was officially stood down took place on Sunday, 3 December 1944 when more than 5,000 men assembled at the Town Hall. Even though the weather was wet and cold, thousands of people collected to see the men of the most remarkable civilian army ever known. They began to collect in the Town Hall Square a full two hours before the parade was due to start. The people lined the route that the march was to take, from the Moor, Rockingham Street and Charlotte Road. A brief service was held in the Drill Hall before Colonel Firth thanked the men of his regiment. He told them:

> Some of you will no doubt feel disappointed that you have not had the opportunity to have any real active engagement, but the fact remains that you have all done the job you were asked to do and done it well. You have my warmest thanks for what you have done and the way you have done it. Continue to be proud of your Regiment and keep up the tradition of service you have established.

Colonel Neill said that many of them were disappointed that the Home Guard was not going to continue to function until the final victory. However, he reminded them that at that very moment the Germans were doing their very best to form a Home Guard based on Britain's own model.

The company then went to the Regent picture house, where the manager Mr Bradley had put up flags to celebrate the occasion. Inside the theatre the atmosphere was more relaxed, as the men chatted and smoked cigarettes and pipes. As the section commander took the stage the band played *If You Were the Only Girl in the World*, to which the audience sang along happily. Once again speeches were made and there were loud shouts and cheers when he especially thanked 'the womenfolk' and the police and other civil defence services. Afterwards the men assembled for the official parade. A reporter stated that 'Their manner of marching, their vigour and smartness made it clear that their patriotic fervour remained bright and undimmed despite the weary years.' The parade of nearly 8,000 men was led by the anti-aircraft regiments from Sheffield, Rotherham and Barnsley and the salute was taken by their commander Colonel Mark Firth and Colonel Neill. Included in the parade were the ladies of the Women's Home Defence Corps headed by Mrs Mackenzie. After lunch at the Town Hall for the officers, a service at the cathedral followed and the opening prayer had the most significant phrase for all those in the audience, which read 'The peril is past, the long watch is over.' The words expressed faithfully the proud spirit of the stand-down parade and the high hopes for the future. The service concluded with a rousing rendition of *Onward Christian Soldiers*.

Despite the deep gratitude that Sheffield people undoubtedly felt towards the Home Guard, the reality was that for four and a half years the men had not been seen as 'real soldiers'. Nevertheless, they had done a very valuable job by acting as sentries and patrolling the countryside, leaving the men of the regular army free to do other work. It has often been said that without them, after the retreat of Dunkirk, the army would not have been able to re-group, re-arm and re-train in order to fight the enemy anew. The fact was that as younger men came of age and left to go into the regular army in preparation for D-Day, more and more men of the Sheffield Home Guard were given extra responsibilities. Undoubtedly they carried out all their duties to the best of their ability and defended the city of Sheffield against a ruthless enemy. Just how ruthless that enemy was, the people of the city were about to find out.

CHAPTER FIVE

The First Air-Raids

A s we have seen, the Germans were aware of the many steelworks that were now producing munitions at Sheffield and they were determined to wipe them out. Nevertheless, as the war progressed it seemed that the bombs were aimed at civilian targets as thousands of houses were hit. Sheffield had a total of 130 alerts and was bombed by German planes on sixteen different occasions between 18 August 1940 and 28 July 1942. Accounts of the raids in the local newspapers, for security reasons, referred to them not as happening specifically in Sheffield but rather in a North Midlands town. Throughout the war the Germans developed even more devastating weapons, like the delayed-action bomb that was designed to explode many hours later. This was aimed to deliberately target the fire, rescue and civil defence personnel as well as ordinary civilians.

Air-raids inevitably left deaths and injuries and the civil defence services were given directions on how to deal with casualties from air-raids. Information about the state of the bodies killed or injured by enemy action was noted in the Sheffield Police General Order Book in July 1943. All officers had to report for duty when the air-raid alarm went off and consequently they were often first on scene at the bombed areas. The book therefore

'Homes not works paid the price of Nazi raids.'

explained what to look out for when trying to rescue trapped persons. It stated that after the bombing a large proportion of deaths would be caused by the collapse of buildings, resulting in 'crush injuries'. Some of the casualties who had been trapped by debris showed little sign of external injury when they were finally released. Many people after being rescued complained of nothing more than stiffness in the muscles around the part of the body that had been trapped. Their general condition appeared to be quite good, but in spite of this shock would develop within a few hours and consequently a large proportion of them died in hospital a few days later. This was due to the absorption of poisonous substances from the damaged muscles or organs of the crushed section. Police officers were instructed to give trapped persons who displayed no sign of injury plenty of liquid (up to four pints) by mouth before they were released from the debris wherever possible. Drinks of hot sweet tea, when it could be obtained, were desirable or failing that just plain water. Injuries from blast again showed no external injuries apart from bruising, which could often disguise more serious internal haemorrhaging. Officers were warned that artificial respiration should not be applied in such cases. The Order Book also described splinter wounds from falling debris, flying glass, blast and ground shock waves. These, once again, caused damage to internal organs that might not be noticed by rescuers due to the small size of the entry wound.

Officers were also instructed how to deal with houses that had received a direct hit. They were urged to give their immediate attention to the less severely damaged houses on either side of the bombed house, or to those across the road where there were walls still standing. The reason for this was that in any partly-demolished house there was a better chance of live casualties being found in rooms where walls offered some protection. Only when they had cleared the other houses of casualties should the officers then give their attention to the house that had received a direct hit. People buried in completely demolished houses had usually been killed outright.

The police, the ARP and civil defence services were ready for the first air-raid attack that appeared over the city at 0020 hours on Sunday, 18 August 1940 when German planes dropped several high-explosive bombs, one landing in the area around Blackbrook Road in the village of Fulwood, Sheffield. Searchlights quickly picked up the bombers and as the anti-aircraft guns sounded, they left in a hurry. Thankfully on that first occasion there were no casualties. Another bomb landed approximately 450 yards south of Redmires Road and penetrated a grass verge, leaving a large crater measuring 30ft by 10ft. Described as being a 'two-street village', many of the houses nearby had been damaged by the blast. One man, a pensioner, was sleeping in his house which was described as standing on its own in a small orchard. The blast blew away the whole of his back wall and also shook all the apples from the trees. He managed to climb down the roof which had been blown off, leaving one edge resting on his bedroom floor and the other in his garden. Two 12-year-old boys next door were quite unhurt in a part of their house that remained intact. They were woken by a whistle just before the blast and calmly told a reporter that they just went next door to sleep.

The bomb damaged an 18in water main and officials and workers from the Water Company were quickly on the scene, inspecting the damage and making arrangements for it to be repaired. As a result of the raid, houses nearby had no water and had to be served by water carts until the pipe had been mended. Warnings were given by vans with loudspeakers that urged householders to boil all water before it was used. Thankfully the water supply was restored at 0620 hours on Tuesday, 20 August. Nevertheless, with this being the first air-raid over the city, the people of Sheffield were anxious to see the damage for themselves. Almost as soon as the cordon was removed around the hole the next day, several hundred persons descended on the area to look at the crater. The following morning there were so many cars that the village was described as resembling a racecourse meeting. One old man aged 74 showed a reporter the damage and said 'I bet there was not one person in this village who was not frightened, but if they think they are going to frighten us with a job like this they are mistaken.'

Other bombs were dropped that night but they fell in open fields, leaving craters stretching out almost in a straight line across the countryside. A householder who lived near to where one of the bombs dropped told a reporter that he and his wife and their two children aged 15 and 6.5 months had to evacuate their house. The police moved them to the safety of a nearby children's home for the rest of the night. Windows and doors had been blown in, and furniture and belongings thrown about inside the properties nearby. Other families whose houses had been damaged were determined to stay in their own homes after the all-clear had sounded, even though the following morning their houses could be seen with gaping holes in the roof and smashed windows.

In the next attack a bomber was seen over the city on the night of Tuesday, 20 August 1940 when he dropped a high-explosive bomb at 2311 hours on Standon Road, Wincobank, Sheffield. Once again the bomb landed on a disused storm bed made up of clinker and slag, which was part of the Sewage Disposal Works near Blackburn Meadows. Nevertheless, nearby houses were again damaged and it was reported that despite the danger, women and children in the nearby houses dealt with the situation in 'a calm and courageous manner.' One family had just gone into their Anderson shelter near to where the bomb fell but they were all unhurt. They stayed inside the shelter until the all-clear sounded. They appeared to be unfazed as they exchanged pleasantries with civil defence workers, busily helping their neighbours whose houses had been damaged. Those who were unable to return to their houses were found accommodation in a nearby school. After the raid there were many complaints because no air-raid warning had been given. Another observer told a reporter that he was lying on his bed with the lights out that night and his bedroom curtains were open. In the sky he saw a solitary plane dive before a deafening crash, followed by a huge flash that lit up the sky.

Later that same night another plane was seen to drop a bomb on open ground at the back of Jepson Road, Wincobank where fourteen houses sustained damage. The whine of the bomb was heard half a mile away and after the explosion nearly all the windows were broken along the entire row of houses. Another family was also determined to stay in their house and spent the night with gaping holes in the roof and windows. The next morning they did their best to make their home habitable again.

The reporter said that 'it was a task to dismay the bravest of housewives, as debris was everywhere and broken glass lay thick in the rooms. Plaster and mortar lay on the kitchen table.' One elderly man told a reporter from the *Sheffield Telegraph and Independent* that he had been sitting in an armchair by the fire when the bomb went off: 'It knocked me and the chair right across the room towards the door, and before I could pick myself up, the plaster from the ceiling hit me on the head.' Another man had just got home from work when he heard the whistling of the bomb and he hurried his family into the Anderson shelter. He said: 'We all got safely into the shelter when the bomb dropped about ten yards away. I could hear it whistling as it dropped and I got my arms around the children. I had no sooner done that than the door of the shelter was blown clean off its hinges.'

The next raid, however, was much more serious and in total there were 4 deaths, 15 seriously injured casualties and 78 less seriously injured. On Thursday, 29 August at approximately 0015 hours several planes were heard flying over Sheffield and the warning was given. A high-explosive bomb was dropped, killing four persons on Sheaf Street and Finlay Street in the St Phillips district of Sheffield. The names of the casualties were Alfred Aspinall aged 65, Edna Winslade aged 15, Douglas Jones aged 23 and an unnamed 15-year-old girl who was hit by flying debris and died a short time later in hospital. Although some shop windows had been smashed, most of the damage had been done to houses. A family in one of them awoke to find their bed in flames, every door broken and the fireplace blown out. Almost immediately after the air-raid warning went off, members of the Home Guard were in attendance at the scene. They were armed with stirrup pumps and buckets of water, even as the enemy planes were still dropping their bombs. About three minutes later men from the AFS had taken over and were dealing directly with the fires. One of the planes could clearly be seen travelling in a north-easterly direction towards the premises of Arthur Lee and Sons at Meadowhall. Once again, a tremendous amount of structural damage was done to houses and it was reported that women and children came out of the bombed houses showing no panic or fuss. An unnamed vicar, on hearing the bombs falling on the houses in his parish, waited until the din ceased before venturing out to visit his parishioners. He offered them sympathy and advice, also telling a reporter that all the windows in his church had been broken, including a very old stained-glass example.

It was ironic in that one of the bombs had damaged a gas main and the next morning one of the workmen praised the Luftwaffe for their service. He told a reporter that the Gas Board had been aware for many years that there was a leak in the area and 'now Jerry has managed to find it for them.' One of those who had a lucky escape was an aged bedridden woman, who had to be lifted to the safety of a nearby school. The next day the Emergency Committee was told that from that one raid 471 persons had been rendered homeless. One of the rest centres was visited by a local reporter the following morning who noted that despite the drama of the previous night, in the corner a row of six children were still tucked into their beds where they appeared to be quite content. One woman told him as she nursed a child on her lap that 'We're still living and that's the main thing.' She said: 'Our roof was blown right off, but we have been luckier than some. My lad's been through Dunkirk and if he can stand things so can I.'

The ARP services worked with commendable efficiency throughout that long night and the following morning. As always, the people of Sheffield were determined to carry on as normal and not let the Germans disrupt their lives.

The next raid took place at 0305 hours on the night of Saturday, 31 August when two high-explosive bombs were dropped on Cookswood Road near Rutland Road, Sheffield. The bomb exploded on impact, demolishing six houses and causing damage to two others, but miraculously there were no fatalities. Once again it seems that the target had been civilians as it was reported that 'there were no objectives of any military or industrial value in the area concerned.' Twenty-three people were slightly injured and three casualties were detained at the Royal Infirmary. For the first time the Germans made use of delayed-action bombs that exploded over the next few days. The worst of these was at 0620 hours the following day when eight police officers were seriously injured and another man was kept in hospital. One of the houses that had been totally demolished belonged to one of their colleagues, a policeman and his bride of just a fortnight who were expected home the next day. It was reported that 'they will find the house they were to live in had gone. Only the bath was left standing on the first floor, which was still visible from the road. All the rest of the furniture for the newlyweds had either been wrecked or blown away in the blast.' A warden who broke his ankle leaping into a trench to escape one of the bombs had no idea that he was only a short distance from a delayed-action explosive. He and twenty of his colleagues had heard two bombs fall, but only one had exploded on impact and they searched for the other. The warden Mr George Hepworth told a reporter that as he got out of the trench and was limping away, 'I did not know I was near the unexploded bomb until there was an explosion and a blinding flash about a dozen yards away from me. I flung myself to the ground and falling debris played a tune on my helmet, but it did not hurt me.'

Another off-duty warden was sitting in his Anderson shelter with his wife and their 3-year-old daughter when one of the bombs exploded on his house. Although none of the occupants were injured inside the shelter, the bomb had thrown dirt halfway up its door and the family had to dig themselves free to get out. Afterwards he reported to his post and took part in the salvage of his own house until his chief ordered him to go off duty. He found that almost all the contents of his house had been broken apart from a few intact eggs that were found in the pantry.

The people of Sheffield were congratulating themselves on their lucky escape when yet another delayed-action bomb exploded six days and fourteen hours after it had been dropped on 29 August. Once again, thankfully there was no one injured. The final delayed-action bomb was dropped at 1635 hours on 4 September at the rear of Grange Cottage, Matthews Lane, Sheffield, causing damage to Norton Grange and a school on Matthews Lane. Despite the upbeat reporting on the courage of people caught in the bombing, the psychological effects must have been very disturbing. A letter written from a woman named Eliza Kate Askew illustrates the fear experienced by many Sheffield people as the bombs rained down. The letter written from her house on Eastgrove Road, Sheffield assures the recipient that they had not suffered much damage apart from frayed nerves. She continues that she:

> simply dreads darkness coming on, for lately the sirens have sounded for four successive nights. We have been straddled with bombs and incendiaries and there is a huge crater three minutes' walk away. The city presents a sad spectacle, and in the outer villages farms have been set on fire and fields

Eliza Askew's letter describing her fear of the bombings.

burnt which had just been threshed. Our ARP wardens said that Nether Haugh women were wonderful in putting out incendiary bombs. No place seems safe and the transport systems are upset, as there are no cars and few buses. It all gets on my nerves. My tummy shakes and also my knees, and I have to hold them to keep still. I go cold all over and the latest thing is an eruption in my head, which the chemist says is due to my nerves.

Eliza Askew was not the only one who dreaded the bombing, but for now there was to be no let-up.

At 0030 hours on 11 September several other bombs fell on different parts of the city. A bomb dropped on Worthing Road killed a woman called Muriel Hall aged 29 while she slept, but both her parents who were also in bed in another room escaped injury. Mr Hall had been an invalid for many years, but he was able to sit up when the emergency ambulance attended just a few moments after the explosion. Both people were rescued, despite the amount of debris that had fallen around them. They were taken to hospital and were reported to be 'recovering although still very seriously injured.' In the peculiar way of bombs, another detonated in the back garden of a house close by in the same neighbourhood on Brett Street the same night. Ironically, although much earth had been displaced by this bomb leaving a small crater, not even a window had been broken. A

Picture askew in a bombed house.

roof of a house was badly damaged and a mattress was found out in the garden. The next day it was reported that a picture was slightly askew, but that was the only damage. A third bomb fell in the yard belonging to Shell Mex premises, leaving a large crater only 15 yards from a petrol tank which thankfully did not explode. Other bombs fell in an area between Tinsley Park Colliery and the city boundary at Bawtry Road. Eight bombs fell in fields and exploded but no damage was done, although forty persons were evacuated from their homes. Another bomb that failed to explode landed south of the washing plant of Nunnery Colliery and was later removed by bomb-disposal experts. An example of the stoicism shown by the people of Sheffield and a determination not to let the bombing get them down was reported the next day. When Reverend R.C. Stevens, the vicar of St Luke's Church, Sheffield saw that his church had been damaged by a bomb, he knew that he had a wedding arranged for the following morning. The bridegroom-to-be was a Dunkirk hero who was in Sheffield on special leave. Reverend Stevens enlisted the help of his wife and other parishioners to clear the church of dust and debris in order for the ceremony to go ahead. He told a reporter that with their help and a good deal of hard work, they finally got the church 'shipshape' and ready for the wedding.

Meanwhile, the raids continued and by now the Germans were using magnetic bombs. These were actually sea mines but they were found to be effective as land-based 'blast' bombs in terms of causing maximum damage. They were dropped by parachute and the ARP Emergency Committee minutes list that some of these were dropped on 20 September on urban areas around Sheffield. The largest of these, measuring 8ft by 2ft 6in, caused a crater 100ft in diameter. They were triggered by magnetic impulses and consequently the ARP workers were asked not to approach any suspected mines wearing steel helmets or carrying steel tools. Ruth Atkin lists the raids in her diary and also notes their impact on her family. On 16 September she reports the bombs falling on the city where one terrific explosion sent them all rushing down into the cellar. She complains that it was such a windy night that several barrage balloons had pulled away from their moorings. These were large balloons or 'blimps' used

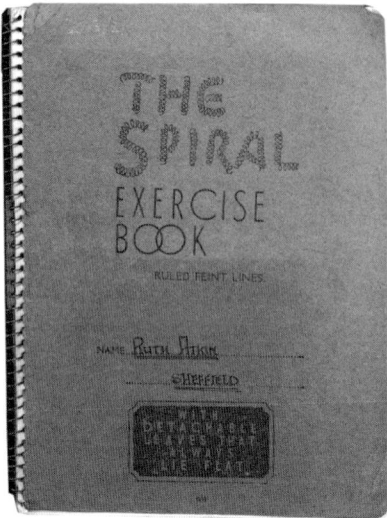

Diary belonging to Ruth Atkin.

for observation purposes or as platforms for communications equipment. They were tethered to the ground with metal cables and one such cable had caught in an electric light wire; as a consequence all the lights in the house kept flickering.

On 26 September three high-explosive bombs were dropped before the warning siren could be given. The planes were spotted at 2123 hours when Gloria Hallett records in her diary that same evening that people watched as three enemy planes flew low over the Wicker. She commented that she 'had never seen planes fly so low.' The bombs caused damage to four houses in Dundas Road, Sheffield but thankfully there were no casualties. Another bomb dropped on Sheffield Road, Tinsley causing extensive damage to four houses from which there were three casualties. The third bomb was dropped on the heat-treatment shop of Messrs W.T. Flather's Standard Works at Tinsley, causing considerable damage to the shop roof but no damage to the vital plant itself. One person was killed and six others severely injured in the incidents at Dundas Road and Sheffield Road and nine persons in total were made homeless. Ruth Atkin's diary also recorded that the three bombs when they dropped 'shook the windows before the sirens went off.' In the sky as she looked out she saw Spitfires attacking the enemy planes and tracer bullets could easily be seen in the sky.

The worst fatality that night occurred when a high-explosive bomb was dropped on four houses in Warley Road, Sheffield. The resident killed was Mrs A. Monks who was preparing to leave her house for the safety of the shelter where her family had slept for the last few weeks. Her two sons were already inside the shelter and Mr and Mrs Monks were about to join them. They were both in the living room when a bomb landed in the back

Sept 12" Nothing heard | 11·20 | | 3 Hrs 20 mins.
" " Planes heard, so down to the | 1 - 5 | W | 1¾
cellar we go. Bombs dropped in | 1·35 | |
the Stocksbridge area. | 2·40 | W | 1hr 5ms
" 13" Peaceful night - no activity over
England apart from a little in
the London district.
" 14" Nothing heard. | 8·35 | |
" 15" No sirens in Sheffield. 185 enemy | 9·30 | W | 55ms
planes down in London area. 25 of
ours lost, but 12 pilots safe - a
record so far | Unexploded time bomb weighing |
| Iron safely removed from front |
| of St. Pauls, buried 26ft in |
| the ground. | 8·10 | |
" 16" Planes heard | 9-0 | W | 50ms.
" " Very windy. Several balloons broke | 10·40 | |
away. One caught an electric | 2·20 | W |
light cable and all lights kept
flickering. No bombs dropped
in Sheffield.
" 18" Quiet night last night - but not | 9·35 | |
| 10·15 | W | 40mins
| 42hrs 35 mins |

Diary entry: 'Very windy. Several balloons broke away.'

garden just outside the shelter. The efficiency of the shelter was tested as the only damage to it was when a brick was dislodged and landed at the feet of one of the two boys. Mrs Monks was hit by a piece of flying metal which also injured her husband and she died shortly afterwards. It was deduced that the last bomb was caused by one enemy pilot approaching from the south and travelling in a north-easterly direction. Another householder a few streets away was upstairs and his wife was in the kitchen when all the windows blew out. Three people were made homeless in

Diary entry, 21 September: '3 big bombs fell.'

that particular raid. The same night a warden on patrol saw some offices where the curtains were blazing at a smashed window. He quickly reached inside and tore the curtains away, and although his hands were burned his quick response prevented more serious damage. Several houses, whose fronts had been blown in, had their occupants evacuated. Rescue workers searching the remains of one of the buildings were amazed to find a dog alive.

He was grimy and black but none the worse for his burial. A short distance away the tenant of one wrecked house was at work when his house was bombed. Thankfully his wife was spending the night at her parents and the first time the couple realized that they had been made homeless was when they turned the corner the following morning and saw just four walls filled with rubble. In another house, the windows had been blown in and the sideboard could clearly be seen swept clean of ornaments. On it and entirely undamaged was a goldfish bowl with its occupant swimming casually around. Nearby a man had been standing near his door when he heard a noise, which he described as 'just a little bang, not very loud but like a firework going off.' Suddenly he found himself sailing through the air, for what felt like miles, before he woke up on the kitchen floor.

On the night of 14 October 1940 a further raid took place when both high-explosive and incendiary bombs were dropped. The bombing started at 2230 hours in the Shiregreen area. One bomb fell on waste ground on Standon Road, only 100 yards from the Barrage Balloon Headquarters, causing a crater 20ft across and 6ft deep. Thankfully there was no damage and no casualties from this incident. However, a delayed-action bomb was dropped on No 8 green of the golf course at Concord Park, but it was only a small-calibre bomb and was quickly made safe by the bomb-disposal squad the following day. Many more bombs fell over the Sheffield area that night, but it was later estimated that most of them were dropped on open ground and consequently caused little damage. Three more bombs landed on private houses leaving damage to roofs and windows, and a fourth dropped on the roof of Woolley Wood Council School on Woolley Wood Road but the civil defence officers made sure that the fires were extinguished quickly. Ruth Atkin reports that night for the first time they slept in the cellar the whole night from 0710 to 0400 hours.

The actions of the ARP services were highly praised by a reporter who accompanied some of them on their work in the city during one of the raids. He stated confidently that:

Sheffield people can sleep comfortably at night confident of the ability, confidence and courage of those men and women who have undertaken voluntarily to guard life against the worst that Goering and his airmen can do. This is not a pious expression of official opinion to uphold the courage of the people; it is the honest to goodness truth, as seen by this reporter who has had the pleasure of watching the Sheffield ARP system at work one night a few weeks ago.

Women ARP workers had been denigrated earlier in the war by being called 'flappers in trousers' by some critics, yet despite this these women worked tirelessly to save lives. After one bad bombing, some of the girl drivers and attendants returned to the station with black faces, as though they had been working in a coal mine for a week. Nevertheless, it was reported that the girls were as cool and collected as ever. When the reporter asked what they had been doing, they replied that they had 'just been helping to get someone out who had been trapped under a beam.' The house had been totally demolished but the men and women had suffered from 'bits' dropping on them as they worked. The reporter watched as they joked about a man who popped his head over the damaged house and asked if the 'all-clear had gone yet' as shrapnel was still clattering onto the roofs. They also laughed about a man who had mysteriously vanished from an ambulance. It seems that he had been wounded in the thigh and had been removed from the shelter into an ambulance. More bombs dropped before it was suddenly noted that he had gone. He was later found back in the very shelter from which he had been removed. The reporter noted his quiet admiration for these women as not one complaint was made about having to drive over shattered glass on the roads, give first-aid to people in the dark, get people out of damaged houses or comfort those whose houses had been wrecked.

As Sheffield was suffering these heavy raids, it was reported that the same thing was happening to the towns of Coventry and Birmingham. It was later thought by the government that these early raids were mainly made for reconnaissance purposes by the Germans and they warned the general public that the worst was yet to come. The people of Sheffield braced themselves for the real thing and it was not long in coming.

CHAPTER SIX

The Sheffield Blitz

Known ever since as the 'Blitz of Sheffield', the nights of 12/13 and 15/16 December 1940 became the most well-documented air-raids over the city. Ironically, at the time of Sheffield's worst bombing raids, many servicemen and women from Sheffield had been sent to London to give nurses and ARP personnel there a well-earned break from the relentless bombing raids they had to endure. One of these was Mrs J. Windle who sent a letter to the *Sheffield Telegraph and Independent* from what she described as being 'the third largest air raid shelter in London' in December 1940. She was a volunteer who had responded to the Red Cross and St John's war organization's appeal for help. Along with a friend from Sheffield, Miss C. Marlow, the two women went to the capital city to work in one of the vast tube stations used as shelters where up to 5,000 people slept every night. In the letter she described how they were able to help. She said: 'There are three very good ambulance men with us and their services are much appreciated by ourselves and the crowd. We arrive about 5 pm and remain until 7.30 am or longer if necessary. Nearly every night we have a "surgery" waiting for us when we arrive on duty.'

Meanwhile, back in Sheffield on the night of 12 December 1940 it was said that the weather conditions were perfect for bomber pilots as the full moon illuminated the city. What made things worse was that the snow on the rooftops also highlighted the many buildings in the city below, which could be seen for miles around. Thankfully, interception of enemy radio had warned the Sheffield authorities beforehand that a raid was planned and consequently the civil defence services were on full alert. It was later estimated that more than 300 planes dropped their bombs over Sheffield as the aerial bombing lasted for over nine hours. People who had spent the many hours in air-raid shelters emerged to find large-scale

Destroyed buildings following the blitz of 12 December 1940.

destruction of the city, and many buildings including hotels, cinemas, churches, shops, industrial premises and warehouses had gone. A second raid took place on 15 December and it was later estimated that in total 602 people had been killed, 513 had been seriously injured and 1,058 slightly injured. It was also estimated that more than 78,000 houses had been damaged. However, out of both these raids came accounts of remarkable bravery from ordinary men and women in the street, police officers, rescue workers and other civil defence teams who worked together to save lives.

On Thursday, 12 December when the air-raid warning went off around 1900 hours, people dashed to the safety of the shelters with no idea of the devastation to come. One man's account of that night was from a chief operator at the Central Picture House on Porter Street, Sheffield, which was later bombed

The remains of the Central Picture House after being bombed.

and destroyed. William Henry Brown told a reporter that a few minutes before 7 pm, the manager Mr Leonard Sullivan went on stage to announce to the audience that the warning siren had gone off. He declared that the show would go on and gave patrons the choice of staying in the building or going down to the air-raid shelter in the basement, which was a former billiard room. Brown finished his shift at 2100 hours and when he went to the billiard room he estimated that there were about 500 people still there. The manager advised them to go to their homes, even though bombs were still being dropped and many of the properties around the cinema were on fire. They left the building in groups of ten and Brown noted that many of them went in the direction of Rockingham Street. Thankfully only a few of them went to the air-raid shelter on Porter Street itself, where later that night there was a direct hit by a high-explosive bomb and many people were killed.

One patron of the same cinema was a woman, just one of thousands of people whose remains were never found. She was an 18-year-old single girl called Sylvia Redfearn, who worked as a shop assistant in Sheffield. At the time of her disappearance she was staying at her married brother's house on Maltravers Terrace on the Wybourne Estate in Sheffield. Her sister-in-law Annie had five weeks previously given birth to a baby and Sylvia had been helping out. At about 1615 hours she left the house to go to the Central Picture House and was never seen again. She might have been killed in the direct hit on Porter Street or she may have tried to make it home; either way she never returned and her family never saw her again. Her parents and two brothers made extensive enquiries at her place of work, Messrs Bevan and Co. of Spital Hill, Sheffield but to no avail. They had the gruesome task of touring mortuaries and viewing many bodies waiting to be identified but never found a trace of her. When her father finally informed the authorities that she was missing, he assured them that she was a very happy girl who was unlikely to have gone off with anyone and had a very good reputation. The family finally approached the Sheffield coroner, Mr A.P. Lockwood in February 1948 in order to have her declared dead, but he advised them to wait until seven years had passed when she would be automatically presumed dead. Identification of many such people killed by a direct hit was very difficult as their remains were often scattered. In order to combat this, ordinary people were buying identity bracelets and having information inscribed on them. In her diary, Gloria Hallett records acquiring a rolled gold bracelet as 'it was deemed advisable in those days to wear means of identifying one self, because bags are so easily stolen.'

Another victim of the blitz was last seen at the Empire theatre; however, he was not a patron but a performer. Edward Kerford was a juggler who worked with his stage partner Roy Billam for twenty years. The pair had been booked at the Empire that week where they were performing, although they lodged at different houses in the city. Kerford and his partner were in the middle of their act that night when the air-raid started. The manager Mr Neale announced that an alert had been heard and the Empire was cleared. The two performers were, with other members of staff, sheltering underneath the stage as bombs were raining down on the city. Suddenly at about 2300 hours Kerford decided to try to make it back to his theatrical lodgings at St Mary's Road, Sheffield. He told his partner Billam 'It's quieter now and I think I will make a break for it and get home to the digs. I will see you in the morning.' The next day when his partner had not turned up, Billam went to St Mary's Road to find all the houses flattened to the ground. Five bodies had been recovered from the ruins, three of which were known to be other theatrical artists who had been identified. However, the other two were impossible to identify. On 14 January 1942 an inquest was held, although the coroner Mr J. Kenyon Parker explained that there was no obligation to hold an enquiry as there was insufficient evidence to certify death. However, he had been requested by Mrs Nora Dorothy Kerford to look into her husband's death in order for her to claim some life insurance money. Kerford's wife gave evidence to say that they had been happily married for ten years and had two daughters who were 9 and 8 years of age. She told the court that 'I have no reason to think that my husband would desert me' and stated that she had not seen him or heard from him since he left to go to appear in Sheffield. Therefore she was convinced that he had been killed in the blitz. She told the inquest that she had placed an advertisement in the *Stage Magazine* on 22 January 1941 asking for any information regarding his whereabouts but had had no response. Mrs Kerford also told the coroner that her husband had not left a will. The coroner was happy to comply with her wishes and Kerford was pronounced dead. He was just one more person who had disappeared during the Sheffield blitz.

The same night, in another incident around midnight five people were trapped in a house and rescue workers and police officers were trying to get them out. A passer-by named Leslie

Harold Currie of Hemper Lane, Greenhill, Sheffield was a sanitation inspector who also volunteered as an animal warden. When he saw the house had been hit by a high-explosive bomb and reduced to ruins, he went to help. He was told that at least five people were still inside and that one man was alive underneath all the debris. Without hesitation Currie, who had a slight frame, crawled into a space where two wooden beams were preventing entry by the more burly rescuers. He was given a saw with which he managed to cut through the wooden joints, propping the debris up above him as he worked. At around 0215 hours Currie finally reached the first victim, a young boy aged about 6 or 7 years who had a broken thigh. Before he could be rescued, Currie was forced to put him into a makeshift splint before passing him through the hole he had made in the debris. Without pause, he continued working away until other victims including a man, a woman and a little girl were also extricated from the remains. Digging down, Currie found the man lying on his back, trapped underneath the wreckage. His head was hanging over a gap and his eyes and mouth were full of plaster and he was only just managing to breathe. Both his arms were trapped under a piano frame that lay over him, his wife lay beneath him and under her was the little girl. Currie managed to fasten a rope around each of the individual victims and the rescuers then pulled them to safety. Sadly one person he could not save was another little boy trapped underneath the beam, although he could see that he was already dead. It was only after Currie had been working for many hours that he was finally persuaded to leave. During the whole of that time, he had been exposed to the danger of the collapse of debris above him. Leslie Currie was awarded a George Medal in March 1941 for his heroism in the rescue. These were special medals that had been instituted by King George VI on 24 September 1940, equating civilian acts of bravery with those of the armed forces. Currie told a reporter that his training as a sanitation inspector had given him knowledge about the construction of buildings and this had been an advantage in the rescue. He described to the reporter how he heard a boy shouting for help and went to get him out. The boy, when rescued, directed the diggers to the part of the cellar where his parents and sister were still trapped.

At the time he received his award, Currie was a married man with a 2-week-old baby girl.

By far the heaviest loss of life experienced that night was in the bombing of the Marples Hotel that was situated at the junction of the High Street and Fitzalan Square, Sheffield. It was estimated that the hotel, which was seven storeys high, had received a direct hit from a heavy-calibre bomb at approximately 11.45 pm. Within seconds the massive building was described as 'a pile of rubble of about 15 feet high.' It was supposed that

Removal of a body from the Marples Hotel.

more than seventy people were killed, although the truth will never be accurately known due to problems with identification. It was recorded that out of all the fatalities, only fourteen bodies could be properly identified. However, sufficient property had been found including identity cards, jewellery, handbags or cigarette lighters to deduce that the majority of the casualties had been women. Before the bombing started, the people inside the building were in a good humour and singing along to popular songs of the day. At some point around 10.45 pm a bomb hit C. & A. Modes Ltd on the opposite side of the road. The blast smashed the windows of the hotel and caused the customers to descend into the cellar for safety.

Rescue teams were called to the wreckage of the Marples Hotel and they dug frantically to try to get people out, but such was the amount of debris that this had to be postponed until the all-clear had been sounded. Other witnesses spoke about hearing the most enormous explosion and rushing outside to find the hotel flattened. One man, Mr Richard William Reading, a Corporation tram inspector of Neill Road, Sheffield could not believe his eyes when he saw what was left of the massive building. When Mr Thomas Wilson heard the news, he rushed to the remains of the Marples Hotel looking for his wife Edith Grace Wilson who was working as a barmaid there. As he watched the rescue workers he saw a man staggering out of the building and holding his bleeding head. Wilson drew the attention of the rescuers to the man and then rushed to the hole from which the man had emerged. He shouted down into the hole and heard voices of other men trapped in the wreckage. Within two or three hours of the rescue starting, seven men had been extracted alive from the ruined building. In the devastation, two of the men walked away and they were never identified, although the five other men who survived gave their names to the rescuers. They were John Watson Kay aged 46 of Boma Road, Trentvale, Stoke on Trent; Ebenezer Tall aged 42 of Clarissa Street, Shoreditch, London; William Wallace King of Arbett Parade, Bristol; and Lionel George Ball of Knowle West, Bristol. The only local man was Edward Riley of Ecclesall Road, Sheffield. The men all told the same story of how they had been trapped in the wreckage of the building and had dug with their hands to make pockets of air in order to breathe through the smoke and dust around them. Throughout the time before their rescue, they reported how they had slipped in and out of unconsciousness due to loss of blood. It was daylight before the heavy work of the removal of the bricks and mortar began the following morning. By the time they had finished, these workmen estimated that they had removed over 1,000 tons of rubble. The work of clearing the debris of the hotel continued over several weeks but there were no more survivors of the bombing.

Some of the bodies that had been taken out of the devastated building were only identifiable from the uniforms they were wearing. An inquest was held on 13 August 1941 into the death of one such airman who had been identified in this manner. The Sheffield coroner Mr J. Kenyon Parker took statements to prove that four RAF men had been at the Marples Hotel on the night it was bombed. The men, who were all 2nd class aircraftmen, were James George Forbes, William Cross McDonald, Thomas Jones and Frank McHugh. Only one of the recovered bodies was in uniform and had an identity disc with the name McHugh on it but the bodies of his three companions were never found. The coroner established that McHugh had come from Wavertree, Liverpool and was 32 years of age. Forbes had been aged 35 and stationed at RAF Norton, Sheffield, although his home address had been at Elgin in Scotland. Jones was 31 and lived at Formby, Liverpool; McDonald was also 31, also stationed at RAF Norton and had lived at High Bronx, Glasgow. At the inquest the coroner read out a letter from the Air Ministry in London dated 27 February 1941 confirming that all four of the men must now be presumed dead.

The heroic deeds undertaken by ordinary people were not long left unrewarded. By March 1941 a total of six George Medals had been awarded to the brave rescuers in the blitz. One of these was an ordinary 58-year-old workman named George Taylor of Greaves Street, Walkley, Sheffield. He was employed by the Sheffield and District Gas Company who during the raids saw holes made in the gasholders by incendiary bombs. Intent on plugging these holes to prevent them from causing an explosion, Mr Taylor led a party of three men twice up the 45ft and 60ft vertical steel ladders to where escaping gas was burning. During the ascent he was so fully occupied that he failed to see the German pilots machine-gunning him and his colleagues as they worked. The *London Gazette* in announcing the award stated that Mr Taylor's 'courage, devotion to duty and leadership were outstanding.' It reported that 'Taylor's work that night made a story of persistent endeavour to save the gas works, and to make the houses in the vicinity less of a target than they would have been if the gas had been allowed to burn.' Taylor himself praised the heroic conduct of his colleagues, namely Messrs J. Oldfield, G. Waller, Plunkett and Gregory.

Rescue workers were still trying to dig out bodies from under the damaged buildings on Saturday, 14 December when news came that the body of well-known businessman and philanthropist Mr George H. Lawrence had been found. When it was made known that an air-raid shelter at the razor blade factory owned by Mr Lawrence had been hit, rescuers rushed to the scene. One of them was Councillor W.G. Stokes who had been a great friend of Mr Lawrence. Just before the war, George Lawrence and Councillor Stokes had holidayed together in France looking at the First World War cemeteries and memorials. Naturally Councillor Stokes caused the news to be sent to Mr Lawrence's father who quickly arrived at the site of the rescue work. When the body of his son was brought out of the wreckage it was unrecognizable, so the elder Mr Lawrence asked the councillor to look at articles in his son's pocket to ensure that it was George. Sadly he was able to identify the body of his son by a penknife found in his pocket inscribed with his name. The news about the death of Mr Lawrence affected many of the authorities and civilians of the city. He had been a good friend to Sheffield and had led a 'rags to riches' life, starting as a seller of newspapers and rising to become the head of the razor blade business. He was well-known for his generosity which extended to other towns and counties of Britain, but he always gave priority to Sheffield charities. He was fond of saying: 'I have made my money in Sheffield and Sheffield will have the benefit of it.' When war broke out, however, he was very sympathetic to the armed forces and time and time again made generous contributions towards funds for soldiers' welfare. Yet it was this very generosity that had killed him in the end. No one was surprised to learn that he had been in the act of taking food to his employees in the works shelter of the factory when he died.

No one was quite prepared on the night of 15 December when a further attack came and it was reported that 'enemy planes came over in continuous waves.' More than 100 bombers including Heinkel 111s and Dornier 17s entered the skies above the city that night. Some of the dropped bombs found a few industrial targets, although they did not disrupt production. Following the bombing a couple called Mr and Mrs Mallison were trapped for almost two days as they tried everything in their power to dig themselves out of the cellar in which they had become buried. They made strenuous efforts but gradually became weaker and it was only when a warden heard their feeble cries that they were finally brought out by rescue workers, many of whom had dug with bare hands to rescue the trapped pair. When they were finally found they were almost unconscious. However, the following day it was reported that Mr Mallison, who was a local businessman, had died and his wife was in a very serious condition.

The next day the clearing-up was in progress when it was reported that despite the damage, the citizens of Sheffield showed that they could 'take it' by their remarkable cheerfulness, unselfish service and co-operation in the difficulties that they faced. Thousands of voluntary workers joined the officials of the Corporation and the police in their tasks. The Bishop of Sheffield Dr Hunter also praised the people of the city for the way in which they had come through their ordeal. Addressing his congregation after the second round of bombing, he said:

Sheffield has had a cruel visitation which has brought into the open the staunch quality of its people. Going around the stricken areas and going into the rest centres, one can only admire the patient endurance of the homeless and the readiness of everyone to help as best they can. I am pleased that clergy and other helpers have opened additional rest centres where and when needed. The strain on our resources over the next few days will be great, but if the same spirit is maintained, and all co-operate with those in authority, we shall get through and carry on the service of the nation.

Once news about losses from the air-raid became known, the people of Sheffield and districts rallied round. Such were the large numbers of people made homeless following the blitz that an appeal was made for any building capable of housing a number of people to be made available. The teachers of High Storrs Grammar School immediately opened the school to admit 500 of the homeless. Over the next few days people from the areas surrounding the school brought parcels of food, clothing and toys for the families living in the schoolrooms. Others offered practical gifts of prams and sundry useful articles. One grocer offered a sack of potatoes and other vegetables for the homeless in order for them to receive at least two hot meals a day. Several telegrams had reached the town following the raids from relatives enquiring about their families and friends. Among them was a telegram received by the Lord Mayor, Councillor Luther F. Milner from the captain and crew of the battleship named after the city, HMS *Sheffield*. He wrote: 'The captain, officers and ship's company have heard with disgust of the indiscriminate bombing of Sheffield, and trust the casualties were not heavy.' The captain concluded with the statement that 'both Sheffields will carry on till victory is achieved.'

It was not just civilians that died during the blitz. The heroism of the civil defence workers was such that many received awards

HMS *Sheffield* whose captain wrote to express the crew's disgust at the bombing of the city.

posthumously. In one single incident six wardens were killed while carrying out their duties. Two other heroes were men of the regular Ambulance Brigade. George Beck of Tapton Bank, Sheffield drove an ambulance and he was killed with his attendant P. Wood of Thorpe House Avenue, Sheffield. Like many other civil defence workers, they lost their lives while trying to save others. Throughout the night, as the bombs continued to fall, they had driven to all parts of the city to rescue and tend to injured persons. They did not return from one call, however, and it was the following morning before their ambulance was found charred and wrecked. The two men were buried the following day: Beck at Crookes Cemetery and Wood at Norton Cemetery.

Another warden who was involved in the rescue of trapped people that night was 34-year-old Leslie Crofts of Coleridge Road, Attercliffe, Sheffield. He was sent to a nearby street after hearing reports that a number of civilians had been trapped in a cellar. There he found a bomb crater of almost 30ft in diameter, under which a fractured gas main was blazing merrily. Defying the flames and digging with his bare hands, Crofts made a tunnel into the cellar large enough to allow three injured people to escape from the debris. He made sure they were safe before returning to the hole where he managed to attend to another two injured persons. Considerable care had to be taken as the debris could have collapsed at any time, burying the trapped victims and Crofts himself. All the time the rescue was being made, enemy bombers, using the blazing crater as a beacon, were dropping bombs nearby. Two police officers were quickly on the scene and helped in the rescue. They spoke highly of Crofts' bravery in the face of fire, bombs and the possibility of being buried alive. He too was awarded a George Medal in March 1941 and was then interviewed by a local reporter. He said that when the raid started he was working as a shunter in the yard of Nunnery Colliery. When the bombs started to fall he went to see if the wardens needed any help. He told the reporter: 'I found there were things needed doing so I buckled to, but I did no more than my duty. I only did what any other warden would do and I regard the award of the George Medal as a tribute to them also, as they all played their part.' Married and with a 1-year-old daughter, Crofts was born in Sheffield and attended the Woodbourne Road Council School before becoming an air-raid warden in September 1938.

Two other first-aid workers who were both killed while on duty were Thomas Paramore aged 35 of Ringinglow Road, Sheffield and a driver called Thomas Wilson. The two men went to the aid of a wounded man, but finding that he was seriously injured they called for an ambulance. Before the vehicle arrived, however, a bomb was dropped on the building where the three men were waiting and Paramore and Wilson were killed. It was said that Paramore sacrificed his own life by throwing himself over the body of the injured man. Both first-aid workers were struck on the head and back by falling masonry and killed outright but thankfully the injured man was saved. He was finally removed to hospital, where it was reported that at that time he was recovering from his injuries. The man acknowledged that he owed his life to Mr Paramore. On Sunday, 4 May 1941 a memorial was unveiled at the Casualty Service Station in honour of the two colleagues who had died together.

Following the two raids the Emergency Committee met every day for the next week instead of their normal monthly meetings in order to aid the city to return to normal as soon as possible. It was reported that when rumours continued to circulate around the city that special recognition was being requested for some of the civil defence workers, a reporter attended one of the meetings. He asked Councillor Asbury for the names of these brave men. The councillor replied that no name would be given as it would be unfair to single out any individual from so many brave acts that had been undertaken by the men and women of Sheffield. During that week the committee meetings were all attended by the Lord Mayor, Councillor Luther Milner, who expressed his sympathy for the relatives of those killed in the blitz. He told the committee:

I think very few of us contemplated when we met a month ago, that we should have to pass through the terrible experiences which have befallen the city. I wish on behalf of the citizens of Sheffield to express to the sorrowing people who have lost their loved ones our very deepest sympathy. It has been my sad experience to attend one or two of the funerals, and I do wish on your behalf to extend to every suffering person in Sheffield our very deepest sympathy.

Hc also praised the work of the civil defence services who throughout the bombing dealt with emergencies in a calm and efficient manner. He told the committee that throughout the raids they proved their worth on the streets that they patrolled, putting out incendiary bombs, searching for casualties and requisitioning the assistance of other services. Out of the thousands of ARP wardens on duty on the two nights of the blitz, it must be considered fortunate that only ten wardens were actually killed on duty when a bomb was dropped on their post in Coleford Road, Sheffield. Another person that attended the Emergency Committee meetings was Lord Harlech, the Regional Commissioner for Civil Defence, who at a meeting held on Friday, 20 December offered his praise to the members of the committee. He also praised the military, the police and all others concerned in the rescue work. He told a reporter that:

> it is exactly a week since I came to the first meeting of the Emergency Committee following the heavy attack of the previous night. I was so anxious to get down to the immediate practical steps necessary to deal with the situation, that I did not take the opportunity to express my deep sympathy with the city of Sheffield on its ordeal.... It is remarkable that so much progress has been made so quickly, and I have nothing but sincere congratulations to offer to you all.

Lord Harlech spoke of his admiration when previously visiting Sheffield on the morning after the raid. He said of the people that 'they were tired but they stayed on top of the job, well organised and getting down to it quickly.' Later, while he was opening a new boys' club he told his audience that two incidents following the bombing had stayed in his mind after his tour of Sheffield. One was while interviewing an employee in the Public Assistance Department who had been bombed out of his house the night before and his offices had been destroyed. The next morning this same man had organized field kitchens to be available in the city at which more than 2,000 people had been fed. Lord Harlech also recalled that on the same day two small boys were walking through the streets singing popular songs at the top of their voices. This inevitably brought a smile to all those passing by and that scene combined all the defiance towards the enemy displayed by the people of Sheffield. He vowed that 'The Germans cannot beat us with all that kind of thing going on.'

Soldiers from other towns in Yorkshire helping the rescue parties.

The committee read a report of the damage and they were told that assistance in the rescue work had been given by civilians, contractors, military units and the Home Guard. They all worked together in an attempt to dig people out and they were joined by eleven civilian rescue squads and soldiers who had been imported from other towns and cities in Yorkshire.

The Emergency Committee was told that during the bombing, although 7,000 people had been reported homeless and others were still coming into the rest centres, the number of casualties was not as high as it might have been. Nevertheless, the centre of Sheffield was a mass of fallen masonry and the transport system was completely disrupted. People had to walk to work and one of these was Charles Simms. In his book *Charlie's War*, he describes that morning after the blitz, walking to work over a distance of about 3 miles. He wrote:

The tram service was disrupted, and did not restart until a few days later. As I came up Barnsley Road there was a loud explosion in the distance. Flames shot up into the sky. I learned later that a gasometer in Grimesthorpe had exploded. It began to get light as I got a little nearer to work.

Charlie Simms described his walk to work after the blitz.

As Sheffield was beginning the clear-up and reorganizing public services, the first thought among many was for the homeless. The Public Assistance staff, who dealt with requests after families had been made homeless, had been inundated with applications. In an unprecedented step they had been told to take individual requests at face value in the absence of more reliable information. As a show of defiance on 16 December, a recital of Handel's *Messiah* took place at the Victoria Hall to massive applause.

On 17 December the Emergency Committee was informed that the rescue work was now abating but that some incidents were still being recorded. One such was from an inquisitive bank clerk who found an unexploded bomb while returning from an errand, which probably saved many people's lives. Approaching the bank, he strode over a pool of water only to stub his toe on something hard. He bent down and felt the outline of a time bomb. He quickly notified the bank manager who cleared the building just minutes before the bomb went off and badly damaged it. Another report was from an off-duty soldier who was going into the city when he passed a damaged public house. To his horror he could see a hand scratching at a hole in the wreckage. He immediately stripped off his jacket and with the help of a passing corporal managed to make the hole big enough to be lowered into, only to find several people trapped. Once again they had just been rescued before the fumes from stores of liquor next door resulted in an explosion. One of the trapped occupants later told a reporter: 'None of us expected to get out alive, but we remained as calm as possible. Nobody seemed to fear death.'

The committee learned that during one of the raids the Mappin Art Gallery had been hit and £10,000 worth of damage had been done to pictures and other works of art. The staff had made the decision that other priceless objects were to be taken to the Derbyshire estate of the Duke of Devonshire for safe-keeping. Some of the treasures that were moved were the Graves collection of ivories, the famous Wilson pictures and other precious Dutch and English paintings. Conservation of the articles was to continue at Derbyshire. A member of staff told a local reporter that the Graves collection had suffered a very near miss when a bomb had exploded within 20 yards of the precious ivories. Thankfully the collection was undamaged. Meanwhile the Germans were reporting in their propaganda that the continuance of the bombing of Sheffield had been cancelled due to bad weather conditions and therefore it had been postponed for the time being. However, on a reconnaissance raid over the town on 18 December they gleefully reported that a quarter of the town was still burning and many other isolated fires were to be seen.

Following the bombing there had been a great response from other local authorities who had heard about the attacks on Sheffield during the two-night devastation. Donations of food and perishable goods had been delivered free of charge by the railway companies for the people of Sheffield in their hour of need. There had also been donations of 2,000 pairs of boots, which had been delivered to Fir Vale Centre for distribution. Meanwhile another 1,500 had been promised and were coming from London.

Such was the devastation of the city that the Emergency Committee agreed that another evacuation of mothers and children should be implemented as soon as possible. By the following day it was announced that 200 persons had left for rest centres outside the city. Travel passes had been issued to seventy adults with children to go to private billets in other areas. In total, 3,776 persons had taken the opportunity to leave the city and by 3 January 1941 this number had risen to include 100 expectant mothers. At the meeting held on 20 December, the committee was informed that bodies were still being extracted from the ruins of the Marples Hotel. There had also been a mass burial of twenty-five bodies arranged to be carried out that morning. On New Year's Eve a further fifty-three unidentified bodies were buried by the Sheffield Corporation. On 26 December the chair Councillor Asbury read out a letter from the king's private secretary, conveying His Majesty's sympathy with the people of Sheffield and requesting a report on the progress made. The letter also intimated that the king would like to visit the city.

There was little doubt that the Sheffield blitz had been devastating for everyone. The local newspaper referred to it as 'The cyclone of Nazi barbarism which struck the city, rocked it to its foundations and passed, leaving a fiercer determination in the hearts of its people, and a spirit of mutual helpfulness of unsuspected depths.'

The special edition of the *All Clear* magazine for the civil defence services that came out in January 1941 paid tribute to the ARP men and women following the bombing. It said:

It is recorded again and again that their very presence inspired the public with confidence. They dealt with incendiary bombs, put out fires with stirrup pumps, sand and other methods. They helped to rescue those trapped under debris, shepherded people from shelters which were in danger, and gave valuable assistance to the homeless. Not the least of their good work was the manner in which they gave encouragement to those who needed it most.

The article concluded that their devotion to duty was a testament to those ordinary men and women who were ready to defend their city in the face of the enemy's actions. Ordinary people were not forgotten either; those who just got through the experience in the best way that they could without descending into panic and confusion. They were also praised in a report submitted to the Emergency Committee, which included a list of casualties from the two 'nights of horror'. It referred to those members of the public who had no specific job to do 'but wait and stay calm, things easier said than done in a blitz.' These were people who sat in cellars and reinforced basements, such as women with little children, listening to the endless hum of planes and the frightening crunch of falling bombs.

Thankfully, those were the worst raids that Sheffield had to endure. There would be further bombing but nothing would compare to the two nights of terror of the Sheffield blitz.

CHAPTER SEVEN

Later Raids

These later raids were more difficult to document as news of what was happening in Sheffield was naturally superseded by larger events happening in the European theatre, which inevitably pushed local news reports into the smaller press columns. What is known is that in the early hours of 16 January 1941 approximately ten to fifteen incendiary bombs were dropped in the Glossop Road and Whitham Road districts but they were quickly extinguished. One of these bombs landed in the grounds of a hospital but was swiftly dealt with by doctors and nurses, assisted by men of the St John's Ambulance Brigade. Another fell through the hospital roof, causing one of the rafters to smoulder, but this was quickly put out by the fire brigade. Although there were many children inside the hospital, not one of them was hurt. This kind of raid proved the efficiency of volunteer men and women fire guards, who with little or no experience of fighting fires adapted themselves to swift action with a sandbag or stirrup pump when required. Four high-explosive bombs were dropped on the centre of the city causing damage to business premises, a newspaper office, the King's Head Hotel and some shops, although there were no casualties. It was thought that only one bomb did any real damage, that being one which fell on the house of Mr Arthur Kedie. He was on duty in a street close by, helping to put out another incendiary fire. The bomb fell through the roof of his house and set fire to the bedroom furniture. It was only discovered when his son left the safety of the Anderson shelter to fetch a bar of chocolate from the house. He smelled something burning and rushed to tell his father and he and a friend, Mr B. Algus, went back to his home to tackle the fire. By the time the fire brigade arrived it had been extinguished, although the two men were drenched in cold water with which, in the dark, they had accidentally sprayed each other.

Wrecked shops and other buildings in Sheffield.

A lesson learned from this particular raid was the need to keep sandbags inside at all costs. Sand from the bags was often used to smother flames and because they had been left outside in the cold weather, they had frozen. Therefore delays were caused by workers having to break up the icy sand with shovels and rakes before it could be used. Thankfully most of the incendiary bombs had not landed on inflammatory materials but rather on the roads and gardens. The hero of the hour from this raid was an unnamed woman who was operating a small ARP switchboard when one of the bombs landed a few yards away. This elderly widow showed little fear as the door to the room was blown off its hinges and the window smashed. Her only companion was a little Scotch terrier which leapt onto her lap, shivering with fright. The woman bravely remained at her post as the crashing of masonry continued, until she was relieved in the early hours. When the Postmaster General heard of this woman's bravery he wrote to all grades of employees, commending them for their courage and determination.

On 4 February 1941, before the alert had chance to sound, a bomb was dropped on a garden in Slayleigh Avenue, Fulwood, Sheffield that damaged two houses. It was described in the local newspapers as 'only a nuisance bomb' that served no military purpose but was seen by the Germans as merely causing harassment to civilians. Nevertheless, this one bomb left a woman dead and five other casualties. Wardens and first-aid parties were quickly on the scene and they found that a visitor to the house, a woman named Mrs Burgess, had been killed outright. Three other persons named Mr and Mrs Pashley and a Mr Dace were taken to hospital. The all-clear sounded just before midnight. As an aftermath to these raids in May 1941 Gloria Hallet records in her diary: 'There is so little left of the city and now practically every suburb has suffered damage. Sunday night's bombing had concentrated on the East end of the town. The three people in our house were forced to shelter under the stairs, expecting every moment to be our last.'

Gloria wrote that the noise of the raid was 'terrific and terrifying' but the only damage occurred when a few windows became cracked and a small hole was made in the roof. By March 1941 the Emergency Committee was struggling. They reported that at that time there were many complaints from people on the waiting lists for glass to replace that damaged in the raids. Temporary measures had been put in place in order for them to continue to live in their homes but City Architect Mr W.G. Davies explained that it was more important to have roofs repaired. There was also a shortage of labour to repair the damaged houses. He told the committee that even if they got all the glass they needed, they could not take men away from the roofing repairs to glaze windows.

A more serious raid took place on 14 March 1941 when a lone raider effected considerable damage on the Southey Estate in Sheffield, leaving several casualties. The weather conditions were favourable to the German pilots and a full moon was shining. Once again ARP officials and first-aid parties were quickly on the scene and the injured were swiftly removed to hospital. The bomb wrecked three houses and damaged many more. It was reported that during this raid eight persons were killed, of which five of the bodies were unidentifiable. A total of twenty-eight others were seriously injured and twenty-six slightly injured. The Emergency Committee heard that following this raid 450 people had been made temporarily homeless and were dealt with at the Sicey Avenue and Wadsley Bridge rest centres. Another bomb was dropped on a little village on the outskirts of the city; this caused some damage but there were no casualties. Several houses were demolished and early reports spoke of two dead; however, this proved to be false. A farmhouse was demolished in another rural district and one person was killed. It was reported the next day that only heavy bursts of firing from the anti-aircraft guns chased away the lone enemy aircraft.

On 9 May 1941 a massive raid took place in which 100 incendiaries and twenty-eight high-explosive bombs were dropped. They landed in the Heeley, Abbeydale, Millhouses and Sharrow areas, leaving about fifty houses uninhabitable. There was also an explosion at Stokes paint works at Heeley, leaving two people killed and thirty-six injured. At approximately 2330 hours on 12 October 1941 two heavy-calibre bombs were dropped and several houses were damaged in Scott Road and Grimesthorpe Road, Sheffield. One of them fell on the junction of Scott Road and Kirton Road, demolishing a Co-operative Society store and causing extensive damage to adjacent houses. Eight people died, including a 17-year-old girl called Edna Tempest who was taken to hospital where she later died of her injuries. Others slightly injured were John E. Marshall aged 65 and Cyril Beaumont aged 33, who were both detained at the hospital and later released. Mr G.W. Robinson aged 50 and Kenneth Robinson aged 17 were allowed to go home after treatment. Another bomb was dropped on Ellesmere Road that demolished three houses numbered 285–9 and eleven persons were trapped under the wreckage. Once again, rescue parties were quickly on the scene and eventually four persons were rescued alive, although two of them died a few days later. The remaining seven were all killed, leaving a total of nine dead and a further nineteen injured. The following day the Town Clerk, Mr E.B. Gibson visited the area at 1500 hours. He reported back to the Emergency Committee the following day, saying that in view of the amount of debris left from the three houses, all of which had no cellars, it was a wonder that anyone had got out alive. The fact that anyone had been brought out at all was thanks to the untiring efforts of the rescue squads involved. The Emergency Committee heard that night that sixty-four adults and seventeen children had been admitted to the Sicey Road Rest Centre as homeless. Within days these families had been billeted and from that raid alone 372 houses had suffered damage.

The Chief Warden Mr Roberts, in attendance at the meeting, stated that the rescue was mainly due to the wardens of Post 3 group E in the north division and in particular to Warden H.K. Sandford. He told the committee that after considerable debris had been thrown up from the remains of number 285, Sandford volunteered to crawl into a small hole that had been made under the kitchen sink. There he was able to rescue three persons found alive inside a small pantry. Mr Roberts stated that one of the reasons Sandford was able to achieve this was because he was of small stature and therefore able to crawl through. He removed loose debris and managed to release a boy named Keith Middleton unharmed. Throughout the rescue the boy was asking him to release his parents first as they were both trapped in the wreckage and were in a worse state than Keith himself. Sandford and the boy continued to remove the rubble and some considerable time later the father was rescued and two hours later his mother was also released. She had been in a very precarious position as one of her legs had been pinned under a large amount of debris.

Mr Roberts continued with his story, relating that about half an hour before Mrs Middleton was released, it was necessary to insist that Sandford should cease his activities as the man was in a complete state of exhaustion. The City Engineer Mr G. Wallis, who also attended the committee, confirmed the devotion to duty displayed by Sandford. He asked that, subject to the approval of the committee, he proposed to submit the facts to the Regional Commission and to enquire about some form of commendation for Sandford. With regard to the Middleton boy, Mr Wallis reported that he was full of praise for the lad and the courage he displayed. He had called out to his parents throughout the rescue, urging them to remain calm and collected for nearly four and a half hours. Also, because he had been rescued first, he was able to give the rescue party detailed information as to where his mother and father were lying and the type of debris that covered them. This information was crucial to the rescue squad in getting them out of the ruined house. Throughout the operation the boy also kept assuring his parents that the squad would soon get them out. The City Engineer stated that Keith Middleton was an inspiration to the rescue squad and he would also like to put his name forward for an appropriate award.

A few nights later on 20 October 1941 there was another raid, in which thankfully no one was killed. It was described thus:

Searchlights swept the sky over a North Midland town last night, as planes passed over at regular intervals. Intermittent gunfire over a wide area was heard above the throbbing of the planes. Distant bomb flashes added to the night's display, but during the first hour there were no reports of any incident.

Nevertheless, the raid had caused many false rumours in all parts of the city. It was said that a German bomber that had been hit by gunfire had landed on a factory and partially destroyed it. The rumours were so prevalent that the police ordered an inquiry, which found no trace of aeroplane fuselage within the wreckage. Officials of the fire brigade stated later that the damage to the building had been caused by four high-explosive bombs as well as incendiary bombs that had hit the premises simultaneously. However, there had been no fatal casualties. Damage had also been caused to a row of houses and their occupants had to spend the early hours of the morning at a

Wreckage of a bombed factory.

rest centre, only returning to their homes the next day to see what could be salvaged. In the suburbs there were many bombs dropped but thankfully these were so quickly extinguished by Fire Guards that they had no time to do any damage or create a target for the bombers.

Incidents that occurred during these bombings later became part of urban history. One was the story of an unnamed woman who was at home while her husband was on duty fire-watching in the city centre when she heard a hammering on her front door. It was a neighbour who had seen that her house was on fire and shouted at her to get her 2-year-old child out of the building. She grabbed the child and was heading for the shelter when she and the neighbour noticed several small incendiary bombs alight in the garden. Dumping the little child unceremoniously on the grass, she and the neighbour proceeded to put out the fires, which were finally extinguished by throwing wet towels on them followed by shovelfuls of earth. The child, who was just learning to talk, told his mummy 'burn, burn, bang'. At the Nether Edge Hospital there were reports, which proved to be true, that during the height of the bombing a baby had been born underneath a bed.

THIS BABY WAS BORN UNDER THE BED

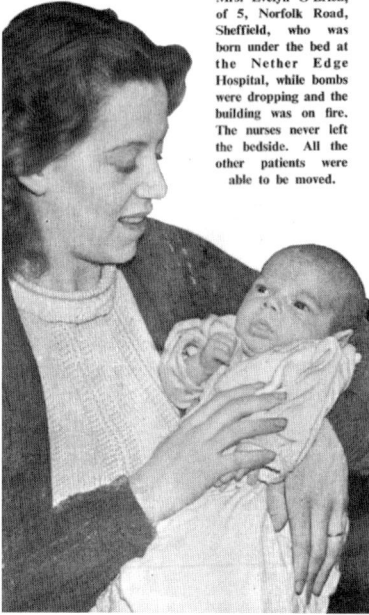

Meet Barrie, the son of Mrs. Evelyn O'Brien, of 5, Norfolk Road, Sheffield, who was born under the bed at the Nether Edge Hospital, while bombs were dropping and the building was on fire. The nurses never left the bedside. All the other patients were able to be moved.

Baby born under a bed at the Nether Edge Hospital.

Another account was that of a 3-year-old girl who had a remarkable escape when the blast from the bomb almost demolished the room in which she was sleeping at the time. Her father Mr Fred Cooper dashed upstairs and groped around in the debris to find his daughter's cot. He finally found it under a large piece of plaster that had prevented other pieces of masonry from falling on the little girl. He cleared away some of the rubble and thankfully found his daughter unharmed apart from a slight cut on her cheek. Her mother told a reporter that she had just finished spring-cleaning and papering the house but added with a smile: 'We still have our lives, and that is everything. We can paper and spring clean again when we have finished with Hitler.'

Although the people of Sheffield did not know it, the worst of the bombing raids was then over. There was only one small incident the following year when incendiaries were dropped at Hunters Bar on the night of 28 July 1942 but they caused only small fires that were quickly extinguished by residents and the NFS. Thankfully there was only one person slightly injured.

In October 1941 the Lord Mayor Elect suggested to the Emergency Committee that a memorial service be held for the victims of the previous year's blitz on Sunday, 14 December at the cathedral. On that day many people gave some thought to those who had died in the air-raids. As late as July 1941 bodies from the December blitz were still being discovered and identified. Four bodies had been found that were believed to be 16-year-old Jessie Hill of Guilthwaite Crescent, Whiston, near

Rotherham; 26-year-old Beatrice Hawksworth of Page Hall Road, Firth Park, Sheffield; 26-year-old Percival Henry Smith of Dansmere Road, Pitsmoor, Sheffield was identified as another; and there was no age recorded for the fourth victim who was James McLardy and was believed to have lived at Sedan Street, Sheffield. All four bodies were found in a passage between two houses when it received a direct hit. It was understood that they were making their way to Firth Park when the bombs began to fall and they turned into the passage to what they hoped would shelter them until after the raid. Like many other families Miss Hill's relatives had made several enquiries at hospitals and mortuaries but nothing could be found about Jessie's whereabouts until her body was discovered.

The accounts of these raids and the heroism of the rescue teams and the people entombed in wreckage gives little indication of what it was really like to be caught in an air-raid. In January 1941 a description of a family's escape from an air-raid in Sheffield was described in a radio broadcast. The 16-year-old Elsie Beever was one of a family of eleven people: her parents, four sisters, four brothers and herself were caught in an air-raid. She described how, when the siren went off at 1840 hours, her father took the children down the cellar steps. They both made the children comfortable before listening to the sounds of the anti-aircraft guns. Against all warnings to the contrary, Elsie went outside and saw the enemy aircraft up in the sky. She could even see a bomb dropping further down the road, blowing in all the windows and several slates from off the roof. Elsie was watching a car being flung into the air before she was shouted at by an air-raid warden who instructed her to go inside. She had only been inside a short while before a bomb went off quite close by and struck the cellar head which made the other children start to cry. The family immediately sought shelter in a neighbour's larger cellar and Elsie carried her little sister who was ill. Throughout the night the two families sheltered without food or water, during which time she and a neighbour managed to put out a fire that had started.

It was quite common for neighbours and families to share large cellars during the raids. Sadly as a result of these cellars becoming a target, multiple members of the same family were often injured or killed. One of the saddest such events took place on the night of the blitz. Once the raid started, Mrs M. Hutchinson immediately went into the reinforced cellar below her living room with her two children, Patricia aged 8 and her son Barrie aged only 4 months. She was joined by her mother, brother and sister who lived next door and her brother-in-law and sister Mr and Mrs Heeley who lived at the other side along with their 9-year-old daughter Barbara. Finally the party was joined by another neighbour who also lived close by. Her husband Mr Hutchinson was a part-time warden and he called in two or three times during that night to make sure the family was safe. At 10.45 pm he was again heading back home and had literally just turned the corner when to his horror he saw a high-explosive bomb demolish all three houses. The bomb fell in the living room of his own house and falling bricks immediately killed little Barrie as he was sitting on his mother's knee. Out of the ten people in the cellar, only Mrs Hutchinson and her brother survived. She later told a reporter that while she was trapped, her right leg was twisted behind her and she had no feeling in it. She was therefore convinced that it had been torn off in the explosion. From the waist upwards she was covered in bricks and debris and could barely move. Finally, after being buried for almost fifteen hours, rescue workers arrived and a shovel was passed to her with which she dug herself out.

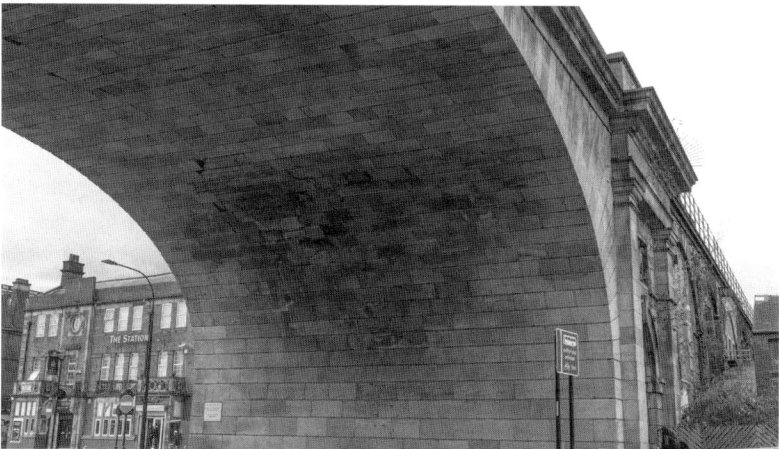

Damage at the Wicker Arches which is still visible today.

The raids in Sheffield were becoming so notorious in the surrounding towns and cities that they were able to learn lessons from the civil defence workers on how to deal with the most severe air-raids. In January 1941 the Sheffield Chamber of Commerce, in conjunction with Superintendent C. Teather of the Sheffield Fire Brigade, sent out an offer to these neighbouring towns and cities offering free training for fire-fighters in Sheffield. During actual raids the men could gain valuable experience while faced with real fires from incendiary and high-explosive bombs. The offer stated that the ability to tackle incendiary bombs swiftly and efficiently was vitally important and proper guidance could be experienced with the men of the Sheffield Fire Brigade. Nevertheless, it must have been a great relief when the tide turned and the bombing finally ceased.

To this very day Sheffield still bears scars from the bombing. Underneath the Wicker Arches can be seen the damage from where an unexploded bomb was extracted. Even the City Hall did not completely escape damage from shrapnel, which can still be seen. Undoubtedly the air-raids remained for a long time in the memory of the ordinary people of Sheffield as they resumed their normal everyday lives.

Shrapnel damage at City Hall which is also still visible.

CHAPTER EIGHT

Sheffield Women at War

The role of women in the Second World War has been fully documented and there is little doubt that it was pivotal to the role of women in today's society. It is safe to say that in this matter Sheffield's women were no different to those in other towns and cities. At the beginning of the war women were limited as to what services they could offer, yet as time went on they gained a freedom never before experienced. When Ernest Bevan declared that 1 million wives were needed early in 1941, there was a great excitement among married Sheffield women who flocked to the steelworks in droves. With the introduction of the National Services Act urging single women to be conscripted to war work, many more found jobs in the steelworks and munitions. The work was hard and they often had to work sixty hours a week for half the pay of the men. Yet, like many other women, when the war ended they were unceremoniously handed their cards and told to return to the domestic sphere. Only today is their work recognized, as Sheffield City Council is launching an appeal to have a bronze statue erected to the 'Women of Steel'. This is a tribute to the women of Sheffield who worked in munitions in dirty, challenging and often dangerous conditions.

Matters started quietly enough on 25 September 1939, when it was reported that the women of the city were organizing themselves by knitting squares to make blankets for bombed-out families. By Christmas they were becoming more organized and even the Lord and Lady Mayoress were helping out. The completed knitted squares were collected by the Mayor, Alderman Longden, using his official car as he distributed the knitted squares to sewing groups to sew them together to make the blankets. His wife the Lady Mayoress also instigated Co-operative Guilds to organize other knitting groups throughout the city. They then went on to make knitted garments for the men serving in the armed forces. Every woman had a role, said one of the councillors, Mrs F.R.S. Moore. She admitted that she herself could not knit but she bought and provided wool for others to use. In the week before the first Christmas of the war, it was announced that the Mistress Cutlers Comfort Fund, combined with an appeal through Sheffield newspapers, resulted in a total of 20,936 parcels containing woollen garments being sent out to the troops. A letter of thanks from the recipient of one of these parcels was printed in the local newspaper dated 5 March 1943 from a Sheffield man who was then a prisoner of war. He wrote that the men from Sheffield, now imprisoned in the same camp, had nothing but praise for the knitted garments that had been sent to them. He told them they were particularly appreciated in temperatures of minus 19 degrees.

Those Sheffield women who were not content to stay at home and knit or make parcels for soldiers but wanted a role in which they could actively help in the war effort joined the civil defence service. By October 1940 women had proved their worth as enthusiastic and competent wardens, yet they still did not seem to have the same role as men. They patrolled the streets as men did, but the women did it in pairs. They were encouraged to make house-to-house calls and help elderly people and invalids. They were also encouraged to assist in fitting gas masks and dealing with the day-to-day problems inevitably brought about by warfare. Once again these lady wardens made themselves invaluable after air-raids where, working in conjunction with the WVS, they could look after minor casualties and young children.

There was something of a breakthrough at Christmas 1939 when it was announced that female workers were needed to help out in a more traditional male role. They were needed to replace the regular postmen that remained. More than 500 women were needed to fill these posts and the postmaster was inundated with applications. Women wearing armbands were now regularly seen around the city and many hoped that there would be more permanent jobs for them after the Christmas period. By August 1940 the Sheffield transport services were asking for another 600 to 700 women to work as conductresses. It was requested that all applicants were to be between 25 and 35 years of age and physically fit enough to climb and descend tram stairs for several hours during their shift. Because of the working hours, however, the post was only open to single women, and mothers with young children were barred from applying. One of the more experienced clippies, who had been working on the trams for five weeks, told a reporter that she loved the job and she preferred male passengers to the females as they 'were much more considerate'. Miss Mildred Saul of Chippinghouse Lane, Sheffield stated that it took some time to learn how to balance properly while the vehicle was in motion. She had found it difficult to keep steady while serving passengers and added that working in the blackout was difficult. However, they had been issued with a small flashlight that could be used for checking money and tickets. Tram inspector Henry Baines said that he had been training conductresses for thirty-three years and found that 'women did this job well during the last war, and today they are doing it equally well.'

One woman who spoke for the ladies of Sheffield was a reporter who had regular articles printed in the *Sheffield Telegraph and Independent* under the title 'A Sheffield Woman's Diary'. Margaret Simpson urged women who were unable to join the services to do what they could to aid the war effort:

> Now the curtain has gone up at last on this drama of war, women have begun to play their important part. Apart from thousands of women who have enrolled in various forms of national service, there are women in every home who can do something to help. Every woman can inspire confidence by words and behaviour in her own small circle. Just being cheerful matters quite a lot, and there is not one woman who has no contribution to make.

Her column continued throughout the war years, expressing what most affected the city women. In December 1939 she was telling her readers that the most 'well-read' book taken out from the library had been *Mein Kampf*, as people struggled to understand the psychology of the man who had plunged the world into conflict. Margaret Simpson also lauded the economy of the Lady Mayoress in February 1940 for setting an example to other women by carrying with her re-usable paper bags for items such as bread when doing her regular shopping. Such was Margaret Simpson's influence that when the 'Diary' suggested that slacks were the best kind of apparel to wear during air-raids, hundreds of women rushed to the shops to buy them. The heaps of slacks, costing from 7s 6d to 9s 11d, were laid out on a shop counter but by that afternoon there were none left.

By July 1940 the women of the city flocked to join the ATS, allowing them to wear uniforms as did servicemen. Now the women of Sheffield truly felt like they were taking an active role, but nevertheless these women initially were still only allowed to work as clerks, storekeepers, clerical workers and cooks. However, what the service did give to women was freedom. ATS workers were billeted together in private houses and for many of them it was the first time they had left home. There were ranks in the ATS that allowed some to be placed in command over other women. One such, who was ranked as junior commander, was a Mrs B. Roberts who was described as a 'jolly, motherly and a very efficient woman.' Margaret Simpson reported that when her 10-year-old son saw his mother dressed in her ATS uniform for the first time in July 1940, he was not impressed. He asked her 'Must you wear that thing?' She replied 'Don't you like my uniform?' to which he added 'Well it will be alright if you're not the only one wearing something like that.' Mrs Roberts said that the women of Sheffield had answered the call for the ATS and they were now enjoying army life. Although at the time many of the girls were being billeted in small private houses, accommodation in several larger houses would soon be available for them. Mrs Roberts showed the reporter one of these larger, comfortable houses in which some of the girls would soon be billeted. Each bedroom held three or four girls and they would sleep on iron beds, straw palliasses and straw pillows, with three army blankets apiece. Mrs Roberts said that each girl would be allowed one photograph and a vase of flowers in the bedroom, as frivolity in the army had to be discouraged. The ages of the women in the ATS were from 17 to 45 and one of them, Section Leader Mrs E. Broadbent told a reporter that she had served in the Land Army in the First World War and had three children, one of them at present serving in the WAAF (Women's Auxiliary Air Force).

On 1 September, two days before the outbreak of war, local newspapers announced that women were needed to join the West Riding Division of the Women's Auxiliary Army Corps based in Bridge Street, Sheffield. It may have been seen as a branch of the regular army, but nevertheless the only positions open to women were in non-combatant roles. It was reported that more than 140 women were needed as telephonists, mess staff, kitchen staff, cooks, equipment assistants, general clerks and a very select few as motor drivers. When it was suggested early in 1941 that these women might be used to deal with the barrage balloons, there was a public outcry. These balloons were essential for protection against low-flying aircraft, forcing them to fly at a much higher altitude where they would be forced into the range of anti-aircraft guns. Although many technical modifications had taken place in balloon-handling and much of the hard manual work had been mechanized, it was still not regarded as a job for women. It was finally agreed that the WAAF of Sheffield would be used to handle the balloons as an experiment for the rest of Britain. They were told that the whole manning policy of the Balloon Command depended on their success. On average the balloons were about 6,000ft high in the air and fairly unwieldy to handle; nevertheless, these women did a spectacular job. The original teams comprised women who were used to working in the balloon repair shops at various centres around the city. They undertook rigorous and lengthy training at Cardington, where the first British airships had been stationed. RAF Norton was selected as the leading

As an experiment, Sheffield women were allowed to work with barrage balloons.

centre for the training of WAAF airwomen in barrage-balloon duties. Some 1,000 WAAF officers, NCOs and airwomen from all over Great Britain came to Sheffield to learn how to work the balloons. Inevitably there was much secrecy around the work of the WAAF and the barrage balloons. The women did a great job and it was only as the war neared its end and the need for inland barrages ceased did the balloon protection of Sheffield come to an end.

Some women preferred to join the WVS which provided them with more traditional

Mrs R.C. Marples of the WVS.

roles. They volunteered to help out serving tea in train stations and buffets or comforting the homeless after they had been bombed out. It may seem to be yet another lowly role, but these women worked tirelessly when needed for very long hours. On the day after the raid of 31 August 1940, Mrs R.C. Marples, a group leader, worked twenty-four hours straight in order to deal with the bombed-out casualties. She had reported for duty at the Ridgeway Road Emergency Feeding Centre at 5 am and very quickly organized twenty other women so that when the homeless arrived they found tables of food and drink laid out for them. Although very tired after her long day's work, Mrs Marples told a reporter that:

One or two wept for the loss of their houses, but I did not see one person who had any sense of hopelessness or despondency. They knew that they would be properly looked after. One of the babies did not take to the milk supplied at the centre, and so one of the officers sent out for ordinary milk and arranged for it to be delivered to the centre every morning until the family had been billeted.

The need for women to replace men who were being called up increased as the authorities searched to find the kinds of industry in which women could take over. In January 1940 it was decided that women could work as laboratory assistants and the appeal was received with much enthusiasm. It had been judged that 'women were more suited to this kind of work, which many girls do particularly well, because it contains intricate measuring and delicate weighing operations.' It was announced that training would be given in various laboratories across the city and the women would have to attend courses at the Applied Science Department of Sheffield University. Many women were also employed at the Fleur de Lis club which served as a recognized rendezvous for men and women of the armed forces. The building on Fargate had been a public house of that name before being rented out on a temporary lease by the City Council. The intention was to provide reduced-cost meals at the centre, where the slogan was 'Hot Meals for Sixpence'. The club was opened by the Lord Mayor, Alderman J.A. Longden on Friday, 15 December 1939 and had been the idea of the Sheffield Christian Temperance Association. A reporter visited

Soldiers at the Fleur de Lis social club.

the Fleur de Lis and said that visitors could order beans on toast with tea for 6d and slices of bread and dripping would only cost ½d. The building was also equipped with comfortable rooms with chairs, sofas and a roaring fire, available for servicemen and women to make themselves at home. With the provision of books, magazines and such luxuries it was hoped that all persons in uniform would have a welcoming place to go in Sheffield. The real advantages of places like the Fleur de Lis were seen in August 1940 when women were serving the local men who had returned from Dunkirk. Many of the women who had tea with the soldiers said 'It was hard to realise that the men who were so jovial in company had stared death in the face on the beaches of Dunkirk just over two months previously.'

Another suggestion made in July 1940 was that it would be suitable for women to drive ambulances. The city authorities requested that young women volunteers take practice runs and study the geography of the district in which they learned to drive. Not only would they be responsible for keeping the ambulances clean, but they would also be given first-aid training and expected to keep records of their journeys. However, one Sheffield woman recorded her initially unsuccessful attempts to undertake such work. Gloria Hallett records in her diary how she volunteered on 1 September 1939 to be a driver for the ARP service, without success. She rushed to enrol but was told by a Mrs Linden that 'only men were really needed'. Nevertheless, Gloria took her own car to a local garage to have the lights blacked out as 'I may be called upon to do night driving.' The following day she was told to report to Hartley Brook Road School but upon arrival Gloria lamented that 'No one seems to know much about me.' After war had been declared, she signed on for full-time service consisting of conveying parties of first-aid workers to their posts after air-raids and other general work. Gloria was very excited as she was issued with a steel helmet and a respirator. On Monday, 4 September there was an air-raid warning at 0335 hours and she rushed for her car to report for duty, but Gloria was disappointed to be told to 'go home'. Two days later she reported again, and was told that 'she was not wanted on site, as it was too dangerous for women.' Completely disappointed, she handed in her equipment and left.

On 11 September Gloria went to the ARP headquarters to see where she stood and a Mrs Ludlam told her that she was surprised she had been sent to the Mobile First Aid section as there 'were no women in that at all'. Gloria had finally made up her mind on Saturday, 25 May 1940, while doing the washing-up, that she was determined to volunteer as an ambulance driver in Sheffield. She vowed to herself that at 40 years of age 'It is time I overcame my slight inferiority complex, after all what others can do, so can I.' On Monday, 27 May Gloria went to see the organizer Mr Hart, who sent her to Coronation Street to see Dr Kerway and become part of his staff. She was delighted to find that she had to take a driving test the following day as she would be starting work that very night. Gloria took the test and admitted to feeling a bit awkward handling four gears of the ambulance instead of the three that she was used to in her 'dear little Morris'. She passed the test and was given papers and told to report to Cedar Lane, Sheffield and there Gloria met 'a very beautiful young man – quite breathtaking in fact.' She was asked to do a 7 am to 3 pm shift that week, with which she was delighted. Gloria was taken into a common room where she met all the other girl ambulance drivers, reflecting ruefully that 'they are all younger than me, and all very bright.' She tried on her new coat which was dark blue with silver buttons, along with a dark blue peaked cap with ARP on it. Sadly on her first shift as soon as the alarm was given, she raced to her ambulance and upon getting inside 'felt something snap in her leg' and was sent home to rest for two days. From then on the diary entries trail off as Gloria was 'too tired to write' and on Friday, 19 July we find out the reason why. It seems that after not writing in her diary for over a month that a certain Jack Driver 'appears to be very devoted'. They had gone out the previous night for a drink at the King's Head and then to the Central Cinema to see Greta Garbo in *Ninotchka*.

Women like Gloria Hallett showed that they were capable of undertaking duties as the equal of men. In the second year of the war, many hundreds of Sheffield women had volunteered to join the Civil Nursing Reserve. These women would be expected to take medical examinations with St John's Ambulance, as well as serve fifty hours undertaking practical training in hospital wards where they would do the work of probationary nurses. During training they were only allowed to feed patients, make beds properly and give assistance to the trained nurses. In the event of an emergency they would be expected to take over the routine hospital work, leaving trained nurses to deal with the casualties. Menial though the work was, they flocked to enrol in such positions.

However, one sphere of work in which Sheffield women did excel, as they did all over the country, was munitions work. In this their marital status was unimportant and for the very first time the local authorities were urging married as well as single girls to enrol. The local newspapers reported the joy of married women who were now able to undertake such war work. An article describing the elation at hearing the news was inserted in the *Sheffield Telegraph* dated 22 June 1941. The article stated that when Mrs Annie Bolland went to see her neighbour Mrs Lizzie Randall, both of whom were aged 37, who lived on Olivet Road, Sheffield she was terribly excited. When she told her friend that she was getting a job the next day, Mrs Randall immediately replied 'Then I am too.' The two women went to the High Street recruitment centre and signed on, both working the same shifts in order that they might travel backwards and forwards together. In that particular recruitment, a total of fifty-seven married women were interviewed for jobs at the munitions factories, many of them having children of school age and husbands either working or serving in the armed forces. Four days later the same newspaper carried pictures of more women working drilling machines in one of the factories. Others were driving trucks and carrying out a task called 'shell roughing'. Under the heading 'Victory depends on Sheffield Steel', the women added that 'they loved working and had met some great pals at the works.' Despite the fact that they were paid lower wages than men, they were often, for the first time, financially independent. These women could earn from £2 3s to £3 10s, although many more made up to £4 or £5 a week. Nevertheless, they had to work long hours as well as undertaking their own domestic chores and caring for their families. The same article proclaimed: 'There are hundreds of women like these in Sheffield. They would laugh at you if you called them heroines, but it is difficult to find another word for them.' Urging that those women unable to work in munitions could still help the war effort by offering childcare to neighbours with children, the article concluded: 'The help of *every* woman is needed during the next few months, because victory depends on Sheffield steel.' The article ended with a question as it asked 'What chance has Hitler got against women of this metal?'

By June 1940 Sheffield women were working on government contracts and a local reporter ran a piece on some more of them. One soldier's wife, Mrs Sally Banks of London Road, Sheffield told him that she had been married for three years. Her husband was away fighting with the Coldstream Guards but when he was given leave, the firm allowed her to spend time with him. Otherwise she worked from 7 am to 7 pm every day apart from Saturday when she finished work at 4 pm. Mrs Banks admitted that she was forced to fit in shopping where she could, either at teatime or after work on Saturdays. Margaret Simpson also admired the women of Sheffield and how they performed their duties as munitions workers. On more than one occasion she was invited to go to one of the works and speak to the women on night duty there. She describes how 'the moon shone palely over the streets, throwing relief onto the terrible grandeur of the bombed buildings' as she made her way to one unnamed factory in September 1940. There she found women workers thrilling to the drama of wartime Sheffield. She wrote: 'Each night they sense the unnamed excitement that comes of being part and parcel of our great national effort. There is a glow in the eyes of girls who look so young in their boiler suits, as the machines whirl and clatter, yielding more and more war material.'

However, from her undoubtedly conservative outlook, she noted that the women had picked up some 'mannish' habits as they drank from mugs and wolfed down a meal at their dinner hour of 2 am. This meal consisted of hot roast beef and a steaming pudding, served by Mrs Mary Woodward who was in charge of the canteen at night. Nevertheless, Margaret Simpson plainly admired these workers, many of whom had to travel miles to work. She stated that when transport was disrupted through the bombing, they were forced to walk up to 7 or 8 miles to complete their shifts at the works. Two single friends from Oak Street, Sheffield, when asked by Margaret if their parents were worried about them working nights, laughed with genuine amusement and told her that they weren't. Dorothy Gratton and Brice Willett said that their parents 'see no danger, no hardship and certainly nothing praiseworthy in what they were doing.' There is little doubt that these women carved out real friendships during the war years, although there was great sadness when one of their colleagues died. Nevertheless, they experienced a previously unknown freedom and sense of worth during this time. With the women working full-time in the factories, there became an urgent need for nurseries to be provided. The Sheffield Education Committee quickly aided the recruitment of married women scheme in July 1940 by finding an extra twenty-three nursery classes to accommodate more than 1,100 children. Added to this were two more wartime nurseries for eighty children and six play centres and plans for more nurseries to open, accommodating up to 800 children. The Education Committee was prepared to spend £6,000 to put nurseries in districts where women were employed in the war industries.

Female workers did have their detractors, however, and the patronizing attitude of some of the men of the period was hard to eradicate. In January 1945 Mr E.H. Hickory of the Iron and Steel Trades Corporation told a reporter: 'The sooner

Tribute from women workers to a colleague who had been killed.

the women get out of the steel industry the happier I shall be. Women have done a grand job during the war, but they could never properly adapt themselves to the steel industry. The work is hot and often arduous.' He added that the average woman, if she were given a decent home to live in and had a husband getting decent wages, would be much happier in the home than in the factory. Mr Hickory concluded with the opinion that factory work was not nearly as nice as people thought it was. As soon as it lost its novelty and interest, women would get fed up with it.

Mr Hickory had his way when it was announced that 150 women employed at Hadfield's, one of the biggest munitions works in Sheffield, were having their contracts terminated in August 1945. A farewell party was thrown for them in the works canteen, where it was reported to have been like the last day at school. The room was filled with bunting and the table groaned beneath ham salad and delicious cakes. Tinned tongue, put away in the days full of the fear of invasion, was finally opened and enjoyed by the partygoers. Tiny flags that had decorated the tables were inserted in the ladies' hair as they cheered, danced, laughed and sang. Many of them were returning home to become housewives once again, such as Mrs Emily Ridley of Aston Street, Sheffield. Aged 48, for the last four years she had worked solidly, one week working days and the following week working nights, varnishing shells and bomb parts. Her husband worked in the building trade, while her son worked in the rolling mills. She told her friends that they had a great welcome waiting for her at home. Other women whose husbands were still in the army chose to continue until they too returned home. One of these was Mrs Rachel Newall of Alfred Road, Sheffield who joined the party in her boiler suit. She had been employed driving a narrow-gauge locomotive since 1941 and intended to continue until her husband was demobbed. The works manager Mr T.W. Melling told the party: 'I was very much opposed to the introduction of women to our works. I could not bring myself to imagine how they could work under conditions which we had. It was with great reluctance that I agreed to their coming.' Mr Melling then admitted to his surprise and admiration at the way the women had tackled the work. On the more repetitive kinds of jobs, he offered his opinion that women stuck to them better than men.

Before the Women's Land Army had been formed, Sheffield women were already volunteering to spend just a few hours a day helping out on local farms. Margaret Simpson in her 'Diary' column was in favour of this, and stated at the end of January 1940 that she had received a letter from a woman whose husband was in the forces. The unnamed writer was urging women to work on farms, saying:

> I myself give four hours each morning to deliver milk, eggs, butter and chickens for a local farmer. In the summer I can do more work, I hope. It is very healthy and good fun and you feel that you are helping with the war effort in some small way.

Once again the farmers were just using the women to deliver goods as if the idea still prevailed that they would only be able to do the light work involved. By 7 November 1940 the more organized Women's Land Army was having great success using voluntary women for all forms of work: driving tractors, managing poultry, milking cows and ploughing. Once the National Service Act was passed, women were then free to join. At first only single women could apply, those between 19 and 43 years of age or widows without children, because of the long hours worked particularly during the summer months. Sheffield women had a choice of either being placed on farms in Derbyshire or they could be sent to work in southern areas. The *Star* newspaper reported that 'Sheffield girls are good land workers.' Lady Anne Hunloke, the County Organizer for the Sheffield Women's Land Army, told a reporter: 'For town girls they have adapted themselves really well to the work. Many of them, now based in the south, had written to the headquarters in Matlock stating how happy they are in their work and also in the comfortable homes which have been provided for them.'

So great had been the response that a Land Army Committee was set up in Sheffield with Mrs Edward Baker as chairperson. She outlined the scheme to a reporter and told him that the position of Land Girl was not a soft option. After enlistment they were given a medical check before being accepted. They were then trained for a month at an agricultural college before being sent out to farms to work on food production. The hours of work generally started from 0530 hours, although in farming terms there were no set hours and the girls had to go early to bed. They worked a forty-eight-hour week and were paid for any overtime. The Land Girls were usually billeted on the actual farm or near to where they would be working, but most farmers ensured that the girls had plenty of spare time. Both the girls and the farmers they worked for were visited regularly by officials from the Land Army Committee and from their opinions it seemed that the scheme was working very successfully. Mrs Baker claimed that each month spent working on the land had increased the physical fitness of the girls and hardened their muscles. One farmer, who had initially been against the scheme, told a reporter that he had found the girls were more conscientious and hard-working than many men. They were organized by the Ministry of Agriculture and although they wore a uniform, they were not considered to be a military force. Nevertheless, these women made it possible for men who had previously been working in agriculture to enlist.

By April 1941 several potential Land Army girls had been recruited from Sheffield. They were starting a month's training at a school at the Silver Hill Nurseries at Ecclesall when Margaret Simpson went to visit them. There she found a girl called Dorothy Castleton busy at work pricking out leeks, onions and tomato plants. Wearing her brand-new uniform, she asked 'I hope you don't mind if I carry on working?' as she busied herself with her task. Dorothy told Margaret Simpson that she was 19 and lived at home at Hillsborough, Sheffield at the moment, but when she finished her training she would probably live away from home. Dorothy delightedly revealed that it was only the second day of her training but she was enjoying the work. Another trainee was Miss Maisie Dawson and she said that she was living with friends in Sheffield and had given up her previous job as a hairdresser to join the Land Army. Maisie said that she preferred horticulture to farming, but she didn't really mind any type of work. A third trainee, Miss Kathleen Hoult of Westbourne Road, Sheffield was also looking forward to making a career on the land after the war. Her sister

Mavis had joined her at the training school; previously both had worked in separate offices but much preferred the outdoor life. Margaret Simpson said that all the girl trainees had 'bright eyes and rosy complexions and they all claimed to be fit and well in the outdoor work they were engaged in.'

It is impossible to list all the tasks that these Sheffield women undertook in order to aid the war effort, illustrating that where there was work to be done, the women of Sheffield were there to do it. They helped with war savings, in a variety of work in the blitzed areas, blood transfusion sessions, toy-making and assembling gas masks. What was not revealed until after the war was how significant Sheffield women had been in sharing Britain's radar triumph. Radar, also called RDF (Range Direction Finder) had been around since the 1930s; however, by the time of the Battle of Britain, the RAF had fully integrated it into all their aircraft. The radio factory of J.G. Graves Ltd at Crookes held 600 people who had been engaged on aircraft radio for more than five years. It was revealed that nine out of every ten workers were women from 14 to 60 years of age. The security aspect was well guarded until late August 1945 when it was revealed that both Sheffield housewives and young girls had been instrumental in supplying those radios. Ex-university technicians were employed to train the women, who did so well that both the Air Ministry and the RAF requested that they be employed full-time. The company was the main contractor for all inter-unit cables for all radio and radar and as a result a large number of Bomber Command aircraft were fitted with the factory's products. Much of the simple elementary work was out-sourced to women working in shops and houses in the area, in groups of fifty or more. In this fashion many Sheffield women contributed to Allied success in the war. The workers of J.G. Graves Ltd were also engaged in the development of the cathode ray for the Air Ministry Research Department. These were later developed for use in television sets and computer monitors. Contracts from the RAF were issued, with modified and improved radar circuits used in the defence of Britain. In recognition of the importance of the work, the award of a British Empire Medal was given to an employee Miss Annie Hall in the birthday honours list.

As in many other cities and towns, Sheffield women's experiences in the war made them even more determined to have a say in local government. They were determined to play a part in post-war events. The National Council for Women decided to send representatives to the Sheffield City Council meetings in June 1943, in the hope that Sheffield would eventually have more women councillors. During wartime there were no elections, so councillors were elected by the council of the same political persuasion as the previous seat owner. Compared to 100 male councillors that year, only eight women were on the council, three of whom represented Burngreave. Their campaign worked and just four months later Mrs L.E. Graham was elected as a Progressive member and the new city councillor for Woodseats. Today there is a wide range of women on Sheffield City Council from different ethnic roots and age groups.

CHAPTER NINE

The Sheffield Police at War

During the lead-up to the outbreak of war, the Chief Constable of Sheffield was Major F.S. James and he quickly realized the effect that the war would have on the city and on his force. Younger men would be called up for service which would decimate his numbers and in order to counter this a total of thirty-two special constables was added to the roster. He also used volunteer constables, who wore the same uniform as the other men with the exception of an epaulette with WRC (War Reserve Constable) added on the collar. Another addition came in August 1939 when the Women's Auxiliary Police Corps was formed for women between the ages of 18 and 55 and they too were added to the squad. Looking at the roles they would perform once again indicates that like many other women workers at the time, they were mainly used as clerks, drivers or as workers in the police canteen. However, Sheffield's local newspapers thought they were an asset to the police service and remarked on the 'admiring glances that were seen on their smart appearance.' At first only fifteen women were recruited, but as the war continued this number increased until by December 1942 there were eighty women working for the Sheffield police force.

Along with their regular duties of keeping the peace and making sure the traffic kept flowing, the force now had extra responsibilities brought about by wartime, including enforcing the blackout, pursuing deserters, control of the air-raid warning system, liaising with military billeting of soldiers, preparation of military routes and piloting of army convoys through the city. Major James was aware that all these duties had to be performed, despite the role being made more difficult by the blackout and petrol restrictions. Apart from their regular training, all the constables now had to learn how to put out incendiary fires and to attend first-aid classes as well as their ordinary training.

Also during the war the Sheffield police service was issued with steel helmets rather than standard police issue helmets. The chief constable was very aware of the extra duties his men had to undertake and on 11 September, a week after war had been declared, he offered his thanks to all members of the regular, auxiliary and special constabularies. He wrote of 'his sincere appreciation of their loyalty and assistance during the past few weeks, and particularly since the outbreak of war.' He told them: 'The future may be even more strenuous, but I know that I can rely upon every man to do his utmost to render the fullest possible service to his fellow people in whatever sphere of assistance which is required.' Major James was in the habit of giving a Christmas greeting to the men and their wives and families in December, and that year he echoed the warning of September. He told them: 'We are now at war, but come what may, I feel that I can rely on and trust all of you to give of your best.'

In July 1939 the Military Training Act was introduced, this being of a temporary nature in case war should break out. The government planned that all males aged 20 to 21 would register for military training for a period of six months, after which they would be transferred to the Army Reserve. At this point those who politically objected to the war should register as conscientious objectors and failure to comply would lead to a fine of not less than £5. Under the Act such persons were called 'militiamen' in order to separate them from the soldiers of the regular army. Major James instructed his men on their responsibilities under this new Act on 21 July 1939. He told them that the military authorities would send for the militiamen in due course and if they chose not to respond to this summons, a constable would have to visit to investigate the reason why. He was instructed at this point to deal politely with the person concerned, and he reminded his men that the man in question was not under arrest at that point but advised the constables to 'encourage him to join his unit.' If, however, he again did not respond, the military unit would regard him as being AWOL (absent without official leave) and the police would then be requested to arrest him and bring him before the Court of Summary Jurisdiction. Major James stated that in the case of a member of the Territorial Army not responding to a summons, he would be dealt with by the military authorities and therefore it would not be an issue for the police.

Once war had been declared on 3 September 1939, Major James issued a notice that all enemy aliens, especially those of German origin, who 'have not already registered with the police, do so immediately at the Sheffield Court House on Castle Street.' This also included all women who had attained German nationality by marriage and they too had to register. That same month a Ministry of Health circular was sent to the chief constable urging that 'all German, Austrian and Czech females were to be removed from any capacity in any institution.' Many of these women were working at the Sheffield hospitals and Major James gave orders that they were to be immediately suspended from their service. The Home Office explained that the term 'alien' now included 'all persons of doubtful loyalty.'

By May 1940 across Britain there was much suspicion and fear of 'fifth columnists' or enemy spies penetrating the systems of government. Therefore the Home Office was urging all chief constables to show more diligence in ensuring the security of police stations. Major James listed on 3 May that from that date onwards, the entrance to the Police Headquarters on Castle Street, Sheffield:

> will be manned 24 hours a day and there will only be access through the main entrance. The Superintendent or the Officer in Charge will have the responsibility for ensuring the gates leading to the archway should always be kept locked. The only reason for them to be unlocked is when access is requested by the CID cars.

At some point during the war it was decided by Military Intelligence that Sheffield would take part in the most important part of homeland security. This was top-secret work and information about it was not released until after the war. Training secret agents was a very hazardous business and Military Intelligence had to be sure that these agents would not talk if caught by the enemy. As part of their training, each 'spy' would be dropped in a location in Sheffield and told to collect certain pieces of information. Unbeknown to the agent, the Security Section of the CID in Sheffield were told of their visit and an officer would be awaiting them on arrival. They would be followed for a few days before a decision was made to have them interrogated. Major James agreed that the first part of the training would be very low key, and this was often carried on at their lodgings and merely involved asking them questions about their activities. In order to step up the severity at some point, one of the officers would say that he was not satisfied and needed the agent to be taken to police headquarters. There a more severe questioning would take place, with more and more pressure put on the agent in an attempt to 'break' them. The object of this was to ensure they would not succumb to Gestapo interrogation. Only when the Security Section was convinced that the agent would not reveal anything of importance would they then disclose that it was all part of the training. After this a de-briefing would take place, in which the police officers would often make suggestions to the agents about ways of not betraying themselves to the enemy. By this method many Allied secret agents owed their life to the training they received at the hands of Sheffield police. After the war the force was highly praised for the vital part they had played in training agents.

Once married women were being used in the employment market in August 1940, it was also reported that forty-seven of the new policewomen were married women whose husbands were serving in the armed forces. Like those serving in munitions work, special arrangements were made so that their periods of leave would coincide. By this time the policewoman's duties had expanded slightly to include dealing with other women, particularly the large numbers employed in the munitions works, and children. Otherwise they were still confined to driving or maintenance of vehicles, working in the operations rooms and dealing with lost property. It was not until December 1941 that three female police constables were appointed to assist the CID in carrying out their duties. Policewoman Helen Gertrude Hobbs was one of the first to start her new duties on 11 December 1941. The following year five more women were also appointed. Boys between the ages of 14 and 17 were used as police auxiliary messengers. They wore a uniform similar to that of soldiers, but dyed black. Their duties involved manning the switchboard, passing on news about burglaries or air-raids and typing out reports from other forces.

Just because there was a war in progress didn't mean that crime would stop and many criminals took advantage of wartime conditions to continue to break the law. One such villain was a 19-year-old man who was a miner. He was arrested and brought before the magistrates' court on Tuesday, 26 November 1940. The chief constable told the court that he had been charged with various shop-breaking and office-breaking offences. The villain showed no remorse as he frankly told the court that he had no intention of going down the pit again and 'I want to rig myself out for Christmas.' He explained that his life up to the beginning of the war had been hard. He had been forced to work knee-deep in water at the pit, and had been forced to live in an overcrowded house 'rife with bugs, black beetles, mice and wood lice.' He was charged along with a 15-year-old boy with breaking into the premises of Burgon and Sons, Main Road, Darnall with intent to steal. It seems that on 15 November 1940 at about 2140 hours Police Constable Garner was on patrol along Main Road when he saw the younger man at the rear of the shop. He also heard a scuffle and felt instinctively that other persons were present. When the man had been arrested and taken to the cells, PC Garner returned to the shop with the owner to see what had been stolen. Inside the premises they found a poker, a glove and a piece of sacking. The house where the ex-miner still lived with his mother was searched and there officers found a large quantity of clothes. The young boy when arrested made a voluntary statement and admitted other offences that he asked to be taken into consideration. He was also charged with two other boys aged 13 and 14 of breaking into the offices of Kirk and Co., Staniforth Road, Sheffield and stealing torches to the value of £2 3s and £36 5s in cash. The gang of young thieves had also broken into Brightside and Carbrook Co-operative Society and stolen wearing apparel worth £50 13s. The man was sent to stand trial at the Quarter Sessions, while the younger boys were sent to be dealt with at the Sheffield Juvenile Court.

Almost as soon as hostilities commenced, blackout restrictions were placed on both street lighting and vehicles. By December 1939 several police constables in the city were reporting that many motorists were 'doctoring' these devices by removing some of the bars in order to get more light than was permitted. In a newspaper report, Major James warned the public that the police 'had been lenient so far' in prosecutions for such offences but 'from now on we shall have to take stronger action.' Nevertheless, the lighting restrictions inevitably caused accidents and just a few days later one of the first victims was 72-year-old Henry Ledger, who was knocked down by a car in Effingham Road, Attercliffe, Sheffield. He was rushed to hospital and made a good recovery, but this was only the first of many such accidents throughout the war years. There were also reductions in shop lighting, which the constables had to watch out for, and they found that many shopkeepers were breaking the rules. Once again in December 1940 Major James stated that some shopkeepers were keeping within the regulations while others were not and they too would be prosecuted. Another more ominous problem caused by the restricted lighting was that lonely stretches of roads outside the city became targets for men accused of molesting women. The chief constable ordered regular patrols in these rural areas to prevent such attacks. The constables of the West Division were ordered to pay particular attention to the lonely road between Four Lane Ends and Norton where a spate of these attacks had been reported.

Throughout the Order Books for the Sheffield police there are hundreds of commendations for the bravery of its officers. One of these was made on 6 September 1940 when Police Constable Judd was commended for 'his courage and promptitude' in rescuing a woman from a burning building. It seems that on the evening of Wednesday, 14 August 1940 PC Judd was on point duty on Fargate when he saw that a fire had broken out at the store room and dark room of photographers Messrs Yates and Henderson. He immediately called out the fire brigade before running to the scene to help. When he was told that a woman was upstairs and trapped in a room near the fire, he did not hesitate. Covering his mouth with a handkerchief, he went up the smoke-filled stairs and found Mrs Alice Davies of

Ellesmere Road, Sheffield in a semi-conscious state against a wall. He helped her down the stairs to safety and into the fresh air before being informed that another girl was also upstairs. He immediately went back to try to rescue her, but before he had gone far he was informed that the girl was safe and outside. Mrs Davies later told a reporter that she had gone upstairs to do some cleaning and had been cleaning a window when she saw flames coming out of the room below. On the way down the stairs she called in to a hairdresser who shared the building and told him and they all left together. At this point she realized that she had left her coat and returned for it. She tried to go back downstairs again but by now the smoke was so thick that she was disoriented and the lack of lights made things much worse. The fumes from burning objects were making her throat sore and she truly felt that she was going to die. Thankfully she then heard a man's voice say 'I am coming' and although she could not see him, she felt someone clasp her arm and help her down the stairs. She told the reporter: 'I don't know what would have happened if he had not come. I am sure he saved my life.' The store room was completely burned out and water damage had gone into the dress shop below, but thankfully in this case no one was hurt. This was just one instance of the many commendations that were noted in the Order Book.

On 13 September 1940 there had been complaints made to the chief constable that certain families were treating the public shelters as extra bedrooms and claiming special places there to the detriment of other users. It was claimed that just because certain families had a public shelter near to their home, they treated it as if it was their own. It was said that they:

troop in, armed with blankets and extra bedding, to bed down for the night with the result that passers by caught in a raid were unable to get in. Some families, not content with monopolising shelters in this way, also make a nuisance to other occupiers by eating fish and chips and leaving the papers scattered around.

Major James condemned the people he called 'shelter sleepers' and stated that public shelters were never constructed for people to move in for the night. He emphasized that they were made for people caught out in the street during an air-raid. As well as carrying out their duties, the chief constable was asked to co-operate in such schemes as National Savings Certificates, raising funds for the war effort. One particular drive took place in Sheffield in August 1940. Major James was asked by the Home Office to involve his men in the scheme. The Home Office remarked: 'We have found in some circles a general reluctance on the part of individual members to participate. This is mainly on the grounds that such contributions paid out of their wages might be taken into consideration in any claims for pay increases.' The circular concluded that there was no substance to this belief, but asked the chief constable to reassure his men should any such reservations come to his attention.

Major James regularly attended the meetings of the Emergency Committee in order to liaise with the Sheffield civil defence services and it was at one of these meetings that he was asked to participate in the 'War Weapons Week' of November 1940. This was due to be opened by the Lord Mayor, Alderman Longden in Fitzalan Square two days later. He was informed that the proceedings would involve two furniture vans, which would be used as selling centres for National Saving Certificates, War Bonds, Defence Bonds and so on. The vans would be open each day from 10 am to 4 pm. Major James was notified that throughout the next week, there would be bands of various military and civil defence units starting from the fairground at 2.15 pm, passing the Town Hall and ending at the cathedral. Drills, displays and parades would also be included to encourage the people of Sheffield to buy the savings certificates. A tank would be on display, and a mobile cinema situated at Barker's Pool. He was informed that throughout the week there would also be other bands parading through the streets of the city, and they would contact the chief constable for permission and to establish their route.

Regarding air-raids, once the warning siren sounded, all police constables reported for duty and all leave was cancelled. Incidents of great heroism from officers of the Sheffield Police were reported to the chief constable during the blitz of 12/13 and 15/16 December 1940 as they joined in with the other rescue services working alongside them. One such heroic act was that of a 27-year-old policeman named Samuel Radford who served in the east part of the city. It was later reported to Major James that Radford had spent five hours during the blitz, while bombs were dropping all around him, tunnelling under smouldering wreckage to save a 19-year-old youth, Joseph Greenwood, who had become trapped in a cellar. The house was one of a number that had been demolished by a bomb and PC Radford learned that many people had been trapped under the wreckage. Mr and Mrs A. Greenwood, their 13-year-old son Harry, Mr Greenwood's daughter-in-law and her 5-year-old daughter and grandson were also ensnared in the cellar after it had been hit by a bomb. They all managed to be rescued but Joseph, who was in a different part of the cellar, was trapped. As Radford tried to free the boy, the pair were in considerable danger from falling masonry, but fires that started around them were put out by the AFS using stirrup pumps as he worked. The young officer was forced to keep putting wet cloths over his mouth to keep out the smoke and fumes during the rescue attempt. Finally, as Radford was almost completely exhausted, he managed to bring the boy out. Just seconds later, the whole cellar and the building were completely engulfed in flames. Major James later described Radford to a reporter as being 'an extremely bashful and reticent young man.' PC Samuel Radford was awarded a George Medal in March 1941 for his brave actions. Major James said that he would not have known about his young constable's deeds but for the statements of other civil defence workers who saw him in action. He stated that he believed there were many other tales of the heroic actions of his constables, but that it was difficult to get to know about them as they simply carried on with their duties. The following night, after news of the award had been made, a reporter found PC Radford on duty patrolling the streets near to the house where he had rescued the boy. He told the reporter: 'I could not leave the boy there. He is safe now so we can just forget it.'

The chief constable recognized the brave actions of his men during the blitz, and in his 1940 Christmas message Major James told them:

The recent experiences that we have had in connection with air raids give special significance to the message from me at this present time, I am anxious that everyone should realise how very much I appreciate the magnificent way in which you have carried out your difficult duties. I have received from many sources appreciative remarks, one of which concluded 'your staff was just wonderful'. I am sure that anything I might add could not be better said.

Despite his praise, one crime that was committed following the blitz was the most objectionable one of looting. In January 1941 four persons were charged with looting in Sheffield and another charged with receiving the goods. Judge Mr Justice Oliver told the court 'This horrible business has got to stop.' He sentenced eight of the offenders to terms of imprisonment from one to ten years. A 32-year-old window-cleaner, a 40-year-old housewife and her 18-year-old son all pleaded guilty to one charge and asked for seven other charges to be taken into consideration. The prisoners were charged with stealing clothing and household effects on 13 December 1940 and in January 1941 from four houses damaged by bombs. The window-cleaner was also charged with stealing from the house of a woman who had been buried for two days under the wreckage, while the rescuers were still at work. In total they had stolen toys, cutlery, carpets, etc. to the value of £124. In sentencing the man to ten years in prison, Justice Oliver told him:

In every case you have preyed on the shattered houses of the poor. You gave up a job of £7 15s a week because the looting paid you better. You have led into this horrible business the two people in the dock with you. This offence is going to be stopped.

Sentencing the woman to eighteen months' imprisonment, he told her that he had taken into consideration the fact that she had been lured into the offence by the man. However, he could not overlook the fact that all the stolen goods had been taken to her house, which had been made an office for looted property. Another 24-year-old man was charged with three cases of looting and was sentenced to seven years' penal servitude.

Two soldiers aged 35 and 42 were also charged with looting from several bombed business premises in Sheffield and stealing four bracelets, two necklaces, a gold tie pin, a pair of gold cuff links, a gold signet ring and fifty cigars between them. When charged, one of the men had answered that it was temptation that had driven him to commit these offences. A police witness told the court that the man was 'too fond of drink and his army record was poor.' The second man stated: 'It was through lack of money and cigarettes that we committed these crimes.' He already had previous charges of housebreaking brought before the court and he too was a very unsatisfactory soldier. Justice Oliver sentenced these men to five years' penal servitude, telling them that the offences were so serious that in wartime the eyes of the law might consider a death sentence or at the very least a term of life imprisonment. He told them both: 'Looting is a terrible offence and it was rendered worse by the fact that both of you are soldiers. It was a cowardly and dastardly thing to do, to loot unprotected premises which had suffered damage due to enemy action.'

Other villains of the war were those who made false claims in order to obtain money from the Public Assistance Board. Provision had been made for those people who had been bombed out to obtain financial assistance as soon as possible. On 18 March 1941 a man and a woman were sentenced to twelve months' and six months' imprisonment respectively for submitting false raid claims. The pair had gone to the Carlisle Street East office, the man claiming to be the woman's father. He stated that his house had been demolished and he had taken another house but asked for £100 to furnish it. He produced an identity card, but the official noted that the name on the card had been altered and called the police. It was found that the couple had already been given £20 using the same story at another office and they were both detained. Mr J.W. Fenoughty, representing the male prisoner, claimed that it seemed impossible that a person could go to the Public Assistance Board and make a statement, sign it and be given £20 in such a manner. Sheffield magistrates, in sentencing the couple, deplored such 'mean and despicable offences'.

It was not just the police constables that carried out sterling work at the time of the blitz. Special constables were also highly praised in January 1941 for their brave actions. Major James told the Emergency Committee that when they were called back to duty following an air-raid warning, many were engaged in keeping order in shelters, while others were more actively involved in the rescue work. The chief constable told the committee that his men had tackled every task required of them without any thought for their own personal safety. One such man was not on duty and in civilian clothing when the alarm went off. He reported for duty nevertheless and immediately took charge of sixty persons in a shelter. Later when he saw that the building above the shelter had caught fire, he conducted them to the safety of another shelter. When that building also caught fire, he led the group, which then comprised 300 persons, to another shelter. He led them in small groups to safety while the bombs continued to rain down. Major James informed the committee that as a consequence of this particular constable's bravery, not a single life had been lost.

Naturally after the blitz his men had to attend coroners' inquests to give evidence when statements taken from police and special constables became essential regarding any identification of remains from the bombing. At an inquest held on 13 August 1941 the coroner Mr Kenyon Parker was told that a direct hit had been made on a house and shop on Pitsmoor Road, Sheffield. As a result the building was left in ruins. The inquest was held on two bodies that had been found in the wreckage. They were the occupier of the shop, 83-year-old Sarah Ann Coggan, and her shop assistant, a woman called Minnie Vernon. Sarah Ann had a house on Glossop Road, but due to the severity of the raid on the night of 12 December she had not attempted to return to her home. A part-time special constable Henry White Pilmer told the inquest that he had been on duty on Pitsmoor Road when he had called at the shop around 9.15 pm. He had known the two women well for many years and he last saw them in the cellar kitchen attached to the shop. He advised them to go to the public shelter on Fox Street, but they refused to leave. Sarah Ann told him that if she was going to die 'she would die in her own shop.' At about 0030 hours he returned and found several adjoining buildings had been demolished by a bomb. Bravely, this special constable tried to dig out any survivors but, as was usual in these cases, a fire broke out. When the fire brigade arrived they pulled him away from the ruins, as by that time nearly the whole row of damaged houses and shops was ablaze. A second witness was James, the brother of Minnie, who told the coroner that he knew Sarah Ann and that she had been the widow of a man called Alfred Coggan. His sister was aged around 50 and was a spinster who worked for and lived with Sarah Ann Coggan. As was usual in such cases, no recognizable remains had been left and it was impossible to make any direct identification, apart from items left in the house. However, the constable's statement and the personal items that were found belonging to Sarah Ann along with some treasury notes were taken by the coroner to be evidential of the two women's deaths. The jury brought in a verdict that the two women had died as a result of enemy action.

By December 1941 Major James had been replaced as Chief Constable of Sheffield by Mr G.S. Lowe and in his Christmas message he told the men and women of the force that 'the welfare of each individual constable is of personal interest to me.' He believed that 'an efficient police force is only possible when there is a complete understanding established between the Chief Constable and all other ranks.' His message was read out to the assembled men and women, along with another Christmas message that had been sent by the Secretary of State at the Home Office, Mr Herbert Morrison. Mr Morrison began by sending greetings to all members of the Sheffield police force, including the members of the Police War Reserves, the special constables, their wives and families, the Women's Auxiliary Corps and the Police Auxiliary Messenger Service. He stated:

Let it be a reminder to us of the things which we are fighting in this war against aggression, lawlessness and tyranny. The Nazi spirit is the antithesis of the Christmas spirit and it will be a sad Christmas indeed for the millions who are at present suffering under Hitler's yoke.

He compared the British trust of our police force to the German distrust of the Gestapo, which he described as 'the tools of a cruel oligarchy, hated and feared even by their own countrymen.'

By February of 1942 the abilities of the constables of the Sheffield police service were held in such high regard that positions in the military services were being recruited through it. Mr Lowe informed his men that the post of Observer (Radio) was open and the RAF was inviting applications from his men. The post required applicants whose education had to be above that of other air crew, and in particular from those who had a quick analytical brain. The post would entail what we now call 'fast-track promotion' and any successful applicant would register immediately as Aircraftman 2nd Class while under training. On commencement of flying training, they would be reclassified as Leading Aircraftman. Once that part of the training was completed, the successful applicant would be promoted to sergeant. The whole of the training would normally be exactly one month after the day they entered the service. Any person applying for the post needed to submit his application to the chief constable who would give consideration to his release from the force.

As part of the officers of Sheffield police's duties were as civil defence observers, they regularly had updates on the types of bombs that might land on the city. Mr Lowe gave his men descriptions of the weapons, what the men should look out for and what steps they should take in reporting these bombs. In August of 1942 he told his officers that when incendiary bombs were seen to fall, it was a matter of absolute urgency that the respective services were notified at once. He urged his men that it was so important that the reporting of such incidents 'must not be postponed until the incendiaries have been dealt with.' He concluded that a very serious view would be taken in cases of failure to promptly report such incidents.

On 3 January 1943 the constables were informed that any British bombs that might have been jettisoned over land by RAF, Allied air force or naval aircraft should also be reported at once. If such bombs were found, the police officer concerned should ensure that adequate safety measures were taken before the arrival of the RAF or the Admiralty bomb disposal units.

On 19 May 1943 the men were told that news had reached the Home Office that Germans were now attaching a spike to certain bombs with the objective of preventing ricochet when dropped from a glider or a low-altitude aircraft. These too must be reported immediately. The next update was the most fearsome one: it was regarding one of Germany's anti-shipping guided missiles that became so familiar over England in the latter part of the war. A description was given of what was called at the time 'a jet-propelled monoplane glide bomb' having a wingspan of 11ft and a length of 9ft. This bomb was described as being 'noiseless in flight, apart from a slight hum.' However, Mr Lowe stated that these were unlikely to be used on land as they were principally intended for attacking shipping. This was inevitably followed by the long-range German rockets that the Germans called V-1 and the British christened 'doodlebugs' or 'buzz bombs'. Chillingly, the first mention of these was made in the Order Book in December 1944 when officers were asked to watch out for them. They were warned that 'they were soundless and the first noise made by these rockets will be in the immediate vicinity of an explosion.' Mr Lowe said that this was usually followed by a reverberation lasting several seconds, which would appear to 'recede into the distance'. The chief constable and the people of Sheffield knew that there was little they could do against such a weapon, which was only finally defeated by the skill of the RAF in shooting them down.

By October 1942 there was a very real fear of invasion and Mr Lowe gave instructions to his officers about invasion protocol and some of the duties they may have had to carry out should enemy invasion occur. It was estimated that officers would have longer periods of duty, so they needed to provide themselves with sufficient food and drink to keep them going for a few days. The chief constable told his men that the first intimation of the possibility of an invasion would be the receipt of a secret coded message. A second message would indicate when the invasion would become likely. Mr Lowe warned them that the duties of each officer were to carry out the functions for which they were organized and equipped, namely to control the civil population. They were to assist the military authorities in controlling the traffic and generally to maintain public order. Firearms or any other forcible means of dealing with enemy marauders could be used against small parties of enemy soldiers, saboteurs or agents. This would apply to any person working on behalf of the enemy who might wish to create local disorder or confusion. The chief constable stated that when individual officers were not working:

> You may hinder and frustrate the enemy by every means which you may devise, or common sense suggests, whilst not impeding the operations of our own defending forces. In this matter, by reason of your training as police officers, and the confidence in which the general public repose in you, you arc specially qualified to provide example and leadership to the general public.

He warned them if an invasion was to occur to make every effort to instruct the citizens of Sheffield to remain in their houses as a matter of utmost importance. Meanwhile, the control of traffic would remain the responsibility of the police officers, and they had to ensure that roads needed for use by the military authorities would be closed to the public. Mr Lowe advocated that vehicles and cycles should be immobilized in order to render them useless to the enemy. However, the destruction of petrol pumps, storage depots, etc. would be the responsibility of owners or the Home Guard to dismantle. Under such circumstances, a watch had to be kept for the subversive elements such as fifth columnists that might deliberately create panic among the people of the city. He concluded by reassuring his men that 'These notices are confidential, and it should not be assumed that the war situation has worsened.'

As we have seen several times throughout the war years, exercises involving the Home Guard and the civil defence teams were important for smooth co-ordination between all the services. In January 1943 these exercises became more serious as they were now needed to develop strategies for how to deal with an actual invasion by the enemy. The exercise was outlined for thc men, along with a reminder from Mr Lowe that the police had the power to close roads to cars and pedestrians, especially those in which live ammunition was to be used. That particular operation was to be called 'Exercise Polar', held on 23 and 24 January 1943, and would be set out in three phases as follows:

Phase One: To commence at 1430 hours on 23 January to 1700 hours when a number of high explosive and incendiary bomb incidents will occur.

Phase Two: Inactive period commencing at 0001 hours on 24 January which will end at 0800 hours during which a military convoy will pass through the city.

Phase Three: Commencing at 0800 hours and ceasing at 1230 hours. This will be an active period of enemy air attack, and involving battles of attacking and defending troops which will include members of the invasion committee.

The chief constable told his men that in order to distinguish between the two sets of troops, it had been agreed that the defending troops would wear steel helmets, whereas the enemy troops would wear field service caps with a white paper band around the front. This would also serve to identify them from troops who were observing and not actually taking part in the exercise. He said that the official spectators would wear red armbands on the left arm. Newspapers later announced that 'Exercise Polar' had been a great success and that substantial advances had been made by all the services involved. However, it was generally agreed that there were a few instances where improvements might be made.

At the beginning of the war it had been announced by the government that there was to be a ban on the ringing of church bells, unless there was an invasion of the country. By March 1943 the fear of invasion was still apparent when officers were informed that if bells should be heard, it was meant to alert a local area of the attempted landing of enemy airborne or seaborne troops. Any such ringing that was heard was not to be taken up by neighbouring church bells. The men were warned that if it was decided that an invasion was taking place, then the decision about the bell-ringing was to be left to the Home

Guard or the military authorities. In the following months, police officers were reminded that if they witnessed an invasion of enemy troops, the information was to be passed immediately to the military authorities by the quickest method possible. All reports should include the time and place where the men had landed, the rank of the informant, the strength of numbers of the enemy, what guns they had with them and if they had any armoured vehicles. The military authorities should also be told whether the enemy had been parachuted from aircraft (including gliders), if they had been engaged by defending forces, and the direction in which the enemy was heading. However, Mr Lowe pointed out that his men needed to make sure of their facts before alerting the military authorities. He explained that if several parachutes were seen descending from a great height, it was probable that the men had ejected from a damaged aircraft.

There were more serious instructions dated 1 July 1943 outlining a police officer's duty when finding a dead body resulting from enemy action. The chief constable told his men that they should immediately write in their pocket book the name and address of the body, the date and time of death, and where and when the body was found. The officer should also record who had identified the body and, if he could, the apparent cause of death. Mr Lowe concluded that if the officer was unsure about the identity of the body, he should include any additional information that might help to name the deceased person. Finally a label should be attached to the body – these were kept in the various police boxes situated throughout the city – prior to its removal. The officer should add his signature to the label. Thankfully, a month later this order was rescinded 'in view of the many other duties' that police officers were required to carry out. It was decided that this particular task should be assigned to the first-aid teams and the ambulance service. From then on, any officer finding a body would simply call out the appropriate teams and give them all the information when they arrived.

On 20 January 1944 the chief constable gave his men instructions on how to approach crashed aircraft for the purposes of obtaining information. They would have to identify the type, number and nationality of the aircraft and pilot to the nearest naval, military, US Army Air Force or RAF station. In cases where the aircraft had crashed with its bombs unreleased, only police officers or civil defence workers who were qualified in bomb recognition were allowed to approach the plane. Only those experts should examine the bombs and decide whether the area was to be evacuated or not. The officers were reminded in March 1944 of the need for secrecy about the 'present military situation and the possibility of future movement of troops.' Mr Lowe recognized that his men were in a particularly good position regarding information on troop movements and he warned them that 'This should not be deliberately or carelessly leaked out and provide the enemy with useful information.' He told them:

AVOID being drawn into conversation about your work or what you have seen or heard.

BEWARE even when discussing what has been printed in the press or through the BBC.

RESIST the temptation to contradict or supplement what others are saying.

DON'T assume that any information is too trivial and that it won't be of interest to the enemy.

NEVER suggest that you have information that is not common knowledge, not even to close relatives.

Sheffield had a prisoner of war camp at Lodge Moor (also known as Redmires Camp) where thousands of German and Italian prisoners were kept. On 3 October 1942 the General Order Book informed police officers that these prisoners were primarily the responsibility of the military authorities and the Home Guard. However, they sometimes fell into the hands of the police and in such circumstances they should be handed over without delay to the nearest military unit. The same arrangement was to be made when captured German officers surrendered themselves to the police. In such a position officers were instructed to search the prisoner and the following should be removed from him: weapons, articles of military equipment, all documents and maps and any effects. The prisoner was to retain only his uniform, identity card, tokens, cash and valuables, his steel helmet, respirator, badges of rank and any war decorations. The articles removed from the prisoner were to be made into a bundle and placed in a sack or a sandbag marked with their name. These were to be handed over, with the prisoner, to the nearest military authority. This was put into practice in November 1944 when a police constable on duty in the early hours of the morning at High Green, Sheffield captured three German prisoners of war. The prisoners claimed that they were all warrant officers and were from each of the three services. The constable told the chief constable that he had found the men on Mortomley Lane, High Green at 12.45 am. He challenged them to produce their identity cards and when he heard the German accent, he took them to his home at Wortley Road, High Green. The men of the Sheffield force previously had instructions as to the treatment of prisoners of war while in police custody, so the unnamed constable would have done his duty while the men were in his care. It was stated in the Order Book that where prisoners had been held for any length of time when waiting for the military authorities to collect them, they should be treated fairly but firmly. They should be given food and drink at mealtimes; however, they should not be allowed to smoke and should be kept segregated from other prisoners and not allowed to speak to their guard. The interrogation of any prisoner would be carried out by experts at Sheffield Police Station or when the prisoner arrived at the nearest military unit. The men were locked up and kept for one and a half hours until an armed motor patrol arrived and took them to Sheffield for interrogation. Afterwards it seemed that the men had escaped from the prisoner of war camp.

Following the Italian surrender in 1943, Italian prisoners of war were treated with more leniency than the German prisoners and many of them worked on local farms where there had been a shortage of labour. Following the rules laid down by the International Convention for the treatment of prisoners of war, the General Order Book gave instructions to officers on how to deal with the Italian prisoners. In Sheffield and district they were still not allowed to fraternize with British troops or members of the public and they only had to have such dealings with them as were necessary to perform the work given to them. Italian prisoners could be allowed to walk or cycle unescorted to their place of work, albeit in parties of less than twelve. However, they were not allowed to 'walk out' unescorted or leave the precinct of their camp or hostel, other than when going backward and forward to work. Italian prisoners were not allowed out on parole and were strictly forbidden to post letters in civilian post boxes. They were also not allowed to enter civilian houses, post offices or public houses; however, they were allowed to enter churches or hospital buildings. Italian prisoners could not have British money in their possession as their pay was issued in tokens that could only be used in the camps or hostels. They were also forbidden to wear civilian clothing.

Finally, following the liberation of France, it seemed that the Second World War might be coming to an end and slowly the Chief Constable of Sheffield began to relax, as reflected in his annual Christmas message of 1944. He wrote:

A large area in Europe has been freed by the armies of the United Nations, and millions of men, women and children will be spending a happier Christmas than they have known for the past five years. The Sheffield Police Service can rightly claim its share in bringing about these great events.... In the latter part of the year, each officer has once more lived up to the high traditions of the Police Service in the part they have played in defeating the enemies' latest efforts to shake the morale of the civil population.

Finally, by May 1945 the people of Sheffield had something to celebrate when Victory in Europe Day was announced. There had been many events planned for Tuesday, 8 May but some of the officers of the Sheffield Police would be on duty that day. It was agreed that they would instead be allowed three extra days' annual leave. For those who were not working, Mr Lowe instructed that 'All ranks are enjoined to act with dignity and restraint, and to avoid any excess in conduct.' He concluded that

'He was confident that the police will bear themselves with the pride in the demeanour for which they are held in high esteem.' His praise was echoed by a message sent by Herbert Morrison to all police services throughout England and Wales. He thanked the men and women for all the innumerable tasks that had been imposed on them because of the war. He added that their role had been made more difficult due to the blackout, which had posed an entirely new problem for the police services. He also praised those members of the force that had served 'and are still serving their country with distinction.' He concluded that it was impossible to celebrate the victory without mention of the many who had given their lives in the service of their country.

Perhaps the last words should be those of the Chief Constable of Sheffield himself, who proudly told his officers:

You have come through the dark days of war with a resounding honour and credit. Its members have contributed to the success of the war in all spheres of National endeavour. I am proud to have commanded such an excellent force of men and women who all, through their service, have shown great devotion to their work and a high sense of duty to the community and their country. The future is full of a mixture of hope and uncertainty. Let us, however, remember our oath and give in the cause of peaceful government so far as it lies within our power, the same honest endeavour and devoted duty as in the days of the war.

CHAPTER TEN

Bombed-Out Families

It is inevitable that war brings chaos to normal family life, and one of the biggest disruptions to life during these years was suffered by people made homeless through the bombings. Many families coming out of the shelters after the all-clear had sounded were stunned to see nothing but rubble, bricks, glass and cement in the place where their homes had been just a few short hours before. The Emergency Committee did its best to help out in such situations. They produced an explanatory leaflet entitled 'What to do if you are made homeless', spelling out what actions such families had to take. The pamphlet took into account the devastation they would experience and stated that 'They believe that the loss of home and all that means will bring a distress which cannot be exaggerated, but which is not irreparable.'

Initially on discovering that their house had been destroyed, such families would be in a clear state of shock. They would be directed by the civil defence services to one of the many rest centres that had been established throughout the city. Upon war being declared, the Emergency Committee had found a number of places that could be used to accommodate up to 3,000 people. Such was the response that almost immediately ten Methodist churches gave their premises over to the feeding and bedding of bombed-out householders. Upon admission to these centres, the family would be offered a hot cup of tea, which was usually found to be very welcome. If the bombing had happened at night, the family might still be dressed in their nightclothes. They would be allocated mattresses or portable beds, issued with sheets and blankets and allowed to sleep for the remainder of the night. The next morning, fresh day clothing would be issued by WVS women who had access to drapery stores. Clothing had been collected from many sources: one in particular was the American Red Cross who, after the blitz,

Bombed-out people trying to salvage what they could from their wrecked houses.

donated approximately 1.5 to 2 tons of clothing. The family would then be in a position to make more practical decisions, such as what they might be able to salvage from their bombed-out home.

After a hot breakfast of sausages, which had been prepared at Fir Vale and sent in hot containers to the centre, sandwiches would be offered to those men and boys who had jobs to go to. Thanks to Mrs Marples and the ladies of the WVS, many of the workers of the city were able to continue with their vital war work. It was reported that even though families had suffered one of the greatest catastrophes that anyone could undergo, they vowed that the bombing would not cost any of the production so necessary in wartime. That night they would return to the rest centre to sleep, but by the next day many of them had already been rehoused. Initially these problems had been dealt with by several co-ordinated groups, but the Sheffield Public Welfare Committee was formed in March 1941 in order to provide help and information at the rest centres for such emergencies. The family would make their claims to the Public Assistance official later in the morning, who would record the names and addresses of people attending the centres. The information on those who had been bombed out was sent to the city architect. He would later visit the property with the city engineer in order to establish which houses could be made habitable by repairs and which would have to be demolished.

A Public Assistance worker listening to a bombed-out woman.

Arrangements were also made by the Corporation to remove the family's goods and larger items of furniture from bombed-out buildings as soon as possible after an air-raid. These were then stored until new accommodation could be found. Supplies of coal were also removed and transported to the family's new property.

The courage of the people of Sheffield was phenomenal following these incidents of being bombed out of their homes. The reports of the Emergency Committee gave an account of actual occurrences following an air-raid. At 0335 hours on 15 October 1940, between sixty and seventy people were taken to the Ridgeway Road Rest Centre and provided with tea and biscuits. Throughout the early hours of the morning they were joined by more people and by 0830 hours there were 222 persons – 64 men, 97 women and 61 children – being provided with hot breakfasts. About 90 per cent of them arrived in their nightclothes and had to be kitted out in donated clothing and footwear. It was noted that being clean and dressed in fresh clothing was very much appreciated and made an instant improvement to their physical wellbeing. It was reported that during such incidents 'The morale of the people was excellent and there was no single instance of hysteria or panic.' In another incident more than 100 people made up of men, women and children arrived at the same centre at 0545 hours. They had been removed from their homes on a Sunday morning during September 1940 after the discovery of a delayed-action bomb that went off at 0615 hours. They were all given hot cross buns and tea and later a cooked breakfast. More continued to arrive throughout the day and by the end of it a total of 308 persons had been dealt with. Usually families arriving at the centre showed no fear and it was reported that the only expressed concern was from a mother who, when arriving at the rest centre, asked the WVS 'Can my little boy have a crayon?' The next day, in another incident, about 100 persons arrived at the Sicey Avenue Centre at 10.00 am following an explosion from a delayed-action bomb that had gone off near Oxford Street Methodist Church schoolroom. ARP officers were sent to the site and removed those people whose houses had been affected and they were directed to the Sicey Avenue Centre. In total, 77 men, 90 women and 68 children were dealt with. A Public Assistance official told a reporter that

the courage of these people has been wonderful. Some have been thrown from their beds and found that the roof of their house has been blown off, but when they came here their chief worry was whether their neighbours were safe. In one case a gable end had been blown off and went through an attic window on the opposite side of the road. We had everything ready for them of course, but the one thing we lacked was a plentiful supply of socks and stockings. Even pets were brought along and cared for. One family of six brought along a dog and a canary. Now they have all found new accommodation. We shall billet the people with private householders until we can re-house them. Whenever possible their own houses are being repaired.

After this raid an appeal went out for furniture and clean clothing for the families that had lost everything and needed to be rehoused. The housing manager, whose offices were opposite

Sorting donated clothes for bombed-out families.

the Norfolk Street entrance of the Town Hall, offered to collect any donated furniture. He had made a list of householders who had room for people who had been bombed out. Their names, addresses and information about how many family members they could accommodate were kept by the authorities at their base at the Central library. Everything had been done to make the families' transition to their new homes easier. Even the telephone numbers for those bombed out of their homes were being quickly adapted. Householders were told that if they informed the telephone supplier of their new address, their calls would be automatically diverted.

Mothers with young children could gain financial assistance to evacuate them to relatives living out of the city centre by obtaining a billeting allowance at the Central library. Those who had jobs in the city had the option of either finding another temporary billet or walking to their workplace every morning. It was a matter of pride to many Sheffielders in such situations that bombed out or not, they never reported late for work. When there had been heavy bombing it was inevitable that the services of water, electricity or gas supplies would suffer. Water carts could be utilized for local families but the gas and electricity supplies were more difficult. Consequently many families were without these services for weeks at a stretch. During one of the bombing raids, the Neepsend Gas Works was practically destroyed and the Effingham Road Gas Works was partly destroyed. Some of the mains that brought coke oven gas into the city were fractured and they took weeks to repair. Thankfully, although both the city's generators were damaged, the supply of electricity was quickly restored. It was a point of pride with the Sheffield Corporation that within a few days of being bombed out, most families would be quickly rehoused. Many of them were extremely grateful and one such person sent a letter to the Sheffield Housing Manager Mr V.M. Hughes, which was read out to the committee of the Lord Mayor's Distress Fund in July 1941. The woman had been rehoused in Shiregreen, Sheffield and said:

> I am writing to thank you from the bottom of my heart. I never expected such a beautiful house. I am a mother who has lived all her life to give her children the best in life. In my home there was everything a boy or girl could wish for, a billiard table and every kind of game that would make them happy. You can imagine after 30 years of married life we had a comfortable home. Imagine then what it felt like to know you didn't have even a cup and saucer or knife and fork. Then two weeks ago today you came along and offered us a house of our own, and to crown it all you offered us blankets and furniture... Believe me it has given me such joy at having a home of my own again, that words cannot express my gratitude.

The letter concluded with the words 'May God bless you all'. Mr Hughes told the Lord Mayor that he had received many such letters, such was the gratitude of bombed-out people. He said that those who had not suffered during the raids could hardly understand the destitution following the loss of all their furniture, clothes and household goods. Many people could salvage very little from their homes after the bombing as most items were not worth repairing. Mr Hughes had visited many of the families after they had been rehoused and found that they had been moved out of squalid houses into much better ones.

One of the biggest schemes to help bombed-out families in Sheffield was introduced to Sheffield City Council by the mayor on 2 December 1940, just ten days before the worst bombing of Sheffield took place. This was a special exchange system whereby families could make their own arrangements about where to go in the event that they should be made homeless. It was called the 'Come Right In Scheme' and was a system of reciprocal arrangements. Families could now volunteer in advance of air-raids to accommodate their friends, should they be bombed out of their houses. It was suggested that the arrangements be made with families who lived at least half a mile away from the bombed area. It also suggested that a bag of clothing and other essentials be left at each other's houses for those involved in the scheme. A booklet was brought out that was dedicated 'to every wife, woman and mother who takes some thought of the morrow and who realises that on her shoulders may fall the responsibilities of caring for those in distress.'

The Lady Mayoress Mrs Lucy Milner told the people assembled at the City Hall that she and the mayor were proud to become the first members of the scheme. She said: 'Never has there been a time when the co-operation of all who are exposed to risk is necessary in order to perfect the arrangements.' Originally the information was stored on index cards naming each member of the scheme and the relatives that had agreed to take them in. However, this was abandoned only days later after the blitz when all the cards had been destroyed. Instead, families were left to make their own arrangements, which seemed to the local authorities to work quite well. It appears that the scheme took off and worked better than anyone had expected; however, there were some detractors. The women of Attercliffe and Darnall held a meeting soon after the scheme had been introduced. At the beginning they had all been in favour; however, some of them did point out the drawbacks. One woman told a reporter from the *Sheffield Telegraph* that:

All my friends and relations live in my own area – in the next street, you might say. I shall certainly find it difficult to find a friend to whom I could go who lives over half a mile away. I think there will be many others in this area like me.

Another complaint was that many of the families lived in small houses themselves, barely adequate to sleep the members of one family, let alone two. Another woman from Attercliffe stated that she had already joined the scheme and had made arrangements to stay with friends at Shirecliffe. She pointed out, however, the disruption her family would have to endure by making the half-hour bus and tram journey to get to work. This disadvantage would be increased by any interruption of transport facilities following a raid. Yet, as she told the reporter: 'If the worst comes to the worst, we are prepared to muck in.' The authorities requested that those people who were forced to leave their damaged houses to stay with relatives should leave a note attached to the front door, or in some other prominent position, giving their temporary address. By November 1941 the scheme was heralded as having helped substantially to reduce the suffering caused by air-raids and had become the basis of a nationwide campaign. The *Sheffield Telegraph* of 18 November 1941 stated that:

In towns and cities all over the country, including London, people are being asked to make arrangements such as were outlined by the Sheffield authority more than a year ago. Films have been made to show the value of friends and relatives having a reciprocal arrangement for shelter after raids.

Mr W. Stansfield, Director of Public Welfare, told a reporter that after the heavy raids on Sheffield, more people went to houses of friends and relatives than had been found billets by the local authority. Nevertheless, the damage to property was immense. Already by 24 May 1941 it was noted in the Emergency Committee minutes that a total of 77,624 houses had been damaged and other options were being considered. The following month it was announced that an inspection had been carried out on a local vicarage to see if a conversion to a hostel for the use of homeless families had been completed.

Sometimes families were not made completely homeless, but due to bomb damage had no cooking facilities as the supply of gas or electricity had been cut off. The solution to this problem was the establishment of feeding centres and the most obvious place to have those was in schools under the authority of the Education Department. However, it was agreed that responsibility for the cost of the equipment and the maintenance of these services would remain with the Ministry of Food. They would provide the financial resources for four cooking depots, municipal emergency rest and feeding centres, and the provision of mobile canteens. Eventually these feeding centres became known as British Restaurants. The Ministry of Food declared that 'Per head of the population, Sheffield is as well served for food as any other town and better served than some.' At that time there were six main feeding centres in the city and fifty-four subsidiary ones in the districts around, all of which worked very hard after the bombing. The scale of charges for meals was deliberately kept very low. In Sheffield prices were on average 1d for a bowl of soup and 5d for a meat and two veg meal. If a person wanted a sweet course they would pay an extra 2d. Sandwiches would be 1½d each and tea would cost 1d a cup. Indeed, these venues proved so popular as places where inexpensive food could be bought that large queues for admission would form throughout the day, which was noted by the Ministry of Food. They stated that the queues in Sheffield were the only ones in the north region and some saw them as quite detrimental. The fact that these feeding centres became so popular during the war was simply because the income of many residents of the city was down to basic subsistence level. Originally designed as 'experimental' centres in areas of great poverty, the December blitz changed all that. After those raids there was an acute shortage of catering facilities in the city centre. Sheffield therefore became the 'laboratory' for which the Ministry of Food developed the Emergency Kitchen Scheme.

The problems for the bombed-out families were eased by the development of such schemes as 'Come Right In' and the establishment of feeding centres, but without the co-operation of the people they simply would not have worked. It may be trite but true to say that in such a position of complete devastation, the fact that neighbours helped each other out in whatever way they could made each individual situation better. The fact that these schemes were readily copied by other towns and cities established the importance of Sheffield as a model to be emulated elsewhere.

Chapter Eleven

Eminent Visitors to the City

When news about the terrible bombing of the Sheffield blitz was heard, many surrounding towns and cities of the West Riding sent representatives to see for themselves. They wanted to understand what services were needed when under such a devastating attack from the enemy. Many were supportive and also sent practical aid ranging from boots and clothing to food, which was transported by rail free of charge. Perhaps the best news that Sheffield received a few days after the blitz was a letter from Buckingham Palace itself. The Lord Mayor, Alderman Luther F. Milner, informed the Emergency Committee on 26 December 1940 that he had been sent a letter from King George VI's private secretary Sir Alexander Hardinge, who wrote:

> The King has been distressed to learn of the damage done to Sheffield by enemy attacks on the civil population. He desires me to express his sincere sympathy with all who have suffered as a result of these raids. It is his Majesty's hope that he may be able to pay a visit to your city before long. In the meantime he would be glad to know how matters are progressing.

True to his word, on Monday, 6 January 1941 the king and queen arrived at Victoria Station, Sheffield where they were greeted by enormous crowds. The couple had arrived in order to carry out a most unusual ceremony. They were met by the Lord Mayor and Lady Mayoress. The queen was described as wearing a dress and coat of Parma violet, the sleeves trimmed with silver fox. Her hat was an exact match for her coat and she wore a diamond brooch shaped like an ivy leaf on her shoulder and four rows of exquisite pearls. A lunch was held at the Town Hall where their Majesties were presented to the Master Cutler Mr W. Woods and other civic dignitaries. On their arrival at the

The king and queen with the mayor and mayoress of Sheffield, Alderman Luther Milner and his wife.

Town Hall the Royal Standard was unfurled and a Union Jack was in pride of place. Mauve tulips and bright yellow daffodils decorated the tables while the king and queen enjoyed a meal of Scotch broth, roast chicken, peas and roast potatoes followed by charlotte de pomme, stilton cheese and coffee.

The royal couple at the feeding centre at St Ann's Road Methodist Church.

After lunch the royal couple went to a feeding centre for homeless people who had been bombed out of their houses at St Ann's Road Methodist Chapel. There they saw voluntary helpers serving sausages and mash that had just arrived from Fir Vale Centre. As the queen watched them eat, she told Mr W. Stansfield, the Centre Officer that 'she felt like crying.' King George saw quite a few people talking to the queen and reminded her gently not to keep them too long or their dinner would go cold. The queen then spoke to the organizers including Mr and Mrs Laking, the minister of St Ann's Church and his wife. They told their royal visitors that they had not changed their clothes in five days and they too were eating and sleeping at the centre. The royal couple was informed that over 10,000 meals had been served at the rest centre since the night of 12/13 December and that everyone had given their utmost to help the homeless people of Sheffield. Many offers of help had been given, ranging from a 76-year-old invalid called Mrs Denton who donated a little electric cooking stove to Lance Corporal Forden who arrived with his team of cooks at the rest centre with their field kitchen. The royal couple then went to another feeding centre at the City Hall where they saw more than 650

Visually-impaired John Wilson talking to the queen and telling her that 'Hitler won't break us.'

people eating their dinner. A few moments earlier the diners had been listening to a loudspeaker playing music, which had been interrupted to inform them of the visit of the king and queen. The royal couple were given a standing ovation before the people returned to their meal of pea soup, bread and two vegetables followed by Christmas pudding. The king was told that such a dinner would cost just 10d. After the meal the king and queen spoke to several people in the dining room. Mr John Wilson, with his wife, both of whom were visually impaired, told the royal couple: 'We can take all that Hitler gives us. He won't break us.' Another man, John Rogan, a steelworker who had been bombed out of his home, told their Majesties: 'They have blown our roof off but we are keeping our pecker up. We shall keep the bulldog spirit.' Mrs Fred Rawlings told the king that along with her husband and ten children they were sleeping and eating at the centre until new accommodation could be found for them. She proudly showed the queen her 6-month-old baby peacefully sleeping in his mother's arms. As the queen left, she told them 'you have all been wonderful.'

Mrs Fred Rawlings proudly shows the queen her 6-month-old baby.

Later the king and queen visited the armaments works of Messrs Thomas Firth and John Brown Ltd in order to carry out the main reason for their visit. This was to be a most unusual ceremony that would take place in the factory: that of conferring a knighthood on the managing director Mr Allen J. Grant. This was probably the first time in history that anyone had been knighted in such a manner. A section of the Sheffield Home Guard formed a guard of honour as the king and queen entered the works. One elderly begrimed workman shouted to the king 'Don't worry owd lad, we'll pull you through' as both their Majesties turned to him with broad smiles on their faces. The ceremony took place on a dais in the Engineering Tool Department that had been decorated with Union Jacks. The spectators were happy to show their approval as they cheered the couple most vigorously when the king placed the sword on Mr Grant's shoulders. The newly-created Sir Allen Grant rose to his feet and the king shook him warmly by the hand. Many of the people who had done sterling work during the blitz then lined up to shake hands with the royal couple, including George Johnson aged 16 and Vincent Clements aged 17. When the queen asked them what they had done, she was modestly told 'We helped to put out incendiaries and fires.' On being reassured that they were not injured, the queen told them that they were very brave. Their Majesties were then shown around the factory and in one department the queen watched a girl called Elsie Chambers at work. The girl was so engaged in the delicate task she was undertaking that for a moment she did not realize the royal visitor was by her side. Wiping her hands down her sides, she told the queen that she 'had started work at the factory at the outbreak of war, and would continue for as long as the work was required.' The whole visit and the knighting ceremony took just three hours but many people felt that it was the highlight of the king and queen's tour.

Following this, the royal couple visited the debris remaining from the bombed houses left after the blitz. It was noted that the queen then wore rubber overshoes in order to walk among the mud and rubble. They were greeted by an enthusiastic crowd who shouted out to the royal couple their determination to win the war. Union Jacks appeared from out of nowhere as the people chanted 'Are we downhearted?' followed by 'No', 'Shall we win?' and 'Yes!' as the couple passed by. One ruined house in particular was that of a Mr and Mrs Dolphin, whose roof had been blown off by the blast. The couple had continued to live in the downstairs part of the damaged house, along with their two sons. When asked by the queen how she was coping, Mrs Dolphin told her: 'We're managing alright thank you, and we are real glad you have come to see us.' The queen surveyed the debris that once had been their homes as she talked to people in the crowd. One woman told her that in the bombing she had lost £50 worth of furniture and had only managed to collect her purse on the night of the bombing. She took it with her to the Anderson shelter and discovered inside the purse the receipt for the furniture, on which she had just paid the final instalment of 6d the day before the raid. She explained that she had built a wall in front of the entrance to the air-raid shelter and it was this that had saved her and her family's lives. She said: 'I made the wall myself, brick by brick. It were a cockeyed wall an' all, but it was OK and saved our lives.' One young man dressed in black told the royal couple that he had lost his wife, child and his mother-in-law as well as his home.

Before the king and queen left the city, they visited another working-class district that had been heavily bombed. The crowd assembled in front of a row of houses on both sides of Coleford Road that was now reduced to rubble. Once again their Majesties were greeted with roars of 'Are we downhearted?' Nearby were the ruins of a church and a wardens' post that had taken a direct hit when ten wardens had been killed and another outside had been injured. The king and queen got out of their car and at once started talking to the people gathered around. One of the saddest figures was the widow of Mr Robert Horace Cooper, one of the wardens killed when the post received the direct hit. The queen, in an intimate chat with her, expressed her sympathy and said how wonderful the spirit of the Sheffield

Thumbs up for the king and queen from the residents of Coleford Road, Sheffield.

people was. Both the royal visitors looked sad as they heard descriptions of the night that the bomb had fallen on the post. They heard how, as people rushed to bring out the injured, one of the last was 57-year-old Mr T. Gascoigne. Although severely injured, he gave the post's documents to his rescuer and asked him to give them to the head warden. These were the last words he uttered as he died immediately afterwards. The royal couple then spoke to a Mr and Mrs J. Evans who had managed to survive the devastation of their house by being in the Anderson shelter as the bomb exploded on their home. Mrs Evans told a reporter afterwards that she did not feel nervous talking to the king and queen, adding 'It was just like talking to any ordinary person.' The king told Chief Constable Major James that they had thoroughly enjoyed their visit and were amazed by the stout-hearted way in which the Sheffield people had endured the bombings. They thanked him for the police arrangements that had been made for their visit. The king told him: 'We know when we come to Sheffield that we shall be perfectly looked after.' During their visit, the royal couple was told that throughout the bombing on the nights of 12/13 and 15/16 December, a total of 668 civilians and 25 servicemen had been killed and more than 40,000 people had been made homeless.

To the civic authorities' great surprise, the king and queen visited Sheffield again on 29 October 1941 when they were en route to Doncaster while visiting four of the largest armament factories in the north of England. It was noted that for a reigning monarch to visit a city twice in one year was unprecedented, and the fact that on both occasions he had brought the queen with him was unique in the history of royal visits. Once again another letter had been received by the mayor from Sir Alexander Hardinge to state that their Majesties would be pleased to meet the mayor, his wife and Corporation officials at the LMS station on that day. Although the visit had been kept secret, the attention of the public had been drawn to the large numbers of waiting police and railway officials gathered at the entrance to the station on the appointed day. Once they were joined by the Lord Mayor and his wife and the town clerk, the people of Sheffield realized that someone very important was due to arrive.

A quarter of an hour later the royal couple arrived in a car to loud cheers. The king was dressed in military uniform as the queen, accompanied by Lord Harewood, walked along a guard of honour of female porters. As the royal couple walked along the line-up, the queen spoke to several of the women. As they entered the station the royal coach was just pulling up to one of the platforms. The queen congratulated the station-master Mr Dixon on the way the station had been renovated since the bombing of the previous December. She also congratulated the mayor on the way the city had been cleaned up since their last visit and the Lady Mayoress for the work being undertaken by the women of Sheffield. While the king and queen were talking to the civic dignitaries, there was a scrabble for tickets to gain access to Platform Two opposite. Those who had been successful crossed over the bridge and had a front row seat as the king and queen climbed into the royal coach that would take them to Doncaster. Their persistence was rewarded when the queen appeared at one of the coach windows and acknowledged the crowd. As the coach pulled away, once again there were loud cheers and applause from the crowd.

The king and queen made a third visit to Sheffield on Tuesday, 25 September 1945 on their way to open the Ladybower Reservoir. It was arranged that they were to drive through the city at just 5 mph in order to give the assembled crowds of adults and schoolchildren a good look at the royal couple. The route they took was along Sheaf Street, High Street, Fargate and Glossop Road to Manchester Road and onto the Rivelin Bridge. There were thirty-four schools whose children were gathered en route, supervised by their teachers. They gave the loudest cheers as the king and queen passed by. The mounted police of Sheffield and the constables lining the route had the hardest job in trying to control the crowd, which surged forward as soon as the royal car was spotted. In consequence a police car with a loudspeaker was forced to go in front of the procession, asking people not to push to the front and impede their Majesties' path.

Another royal figure who made several visits to Sheffield during the war years was Mary, Princess Royal, Countess of Harewood and her husband, Viscount Lascelles. They too first visited Sheffield on 30 December 1940, just after the blitz. The people of the city were not told about the visit at the request of the two eminent visitors in order that they could see for themselves the devastation. Like the king and queen, they too were immediately struck by the resilience and courage of the Sheffield people. During their visit the Princess Royal and her husband left their car and walked through the streets in order to see the devastation for themselves. They walked among city workers and shoppers who thronged the pavements, rubbing shoulders with people, many of whom were unaware of their famous visitors. Although there were no cheering crowds or flag-waving, several people recognized the Lord Mayor and police officials walking alongside the couple and they stopped to stare and wonder. At one point the Princess Royal went into a restaurant where people were queuing before carrying their food into the dining room; the Lord Mayor became separated from the royal party and was forced to converse over the heads of the people queuing up to be served. The couple then visited the Central kitchen at the Fir Vale Centre before talking to occupiers of cottages damaged in the bombing. As they left they expressed their unreserved admiration for the way in which the authorities and voluntary bodies had dealt with the emergency. They also visited the WVS headquarters and the Princess Royal stated 'This is a marvellous sight' as she saw the tables heaped with clothes, boots and blankets that had been donated for use by the city's homeless.

The Princess Royal returned to Sheffield on Tuesday, 15 April 1941 in her role as commandant of the ATS and spent a busy day inspecting billets, visiting a convalescent home and watching members of the Central Hospital Supply Service sorting clothes. The princess, wearing her uniform, was met on arrival by the Officer Commanding the section and given a royal salute by a guard of honour. She was then shown around the different sections of the ATS and stated that she was amazed at the amount of work being done by Sheffield women. After lunching with the officers of the unit, she went to the convalescent hospital where she met the matron, Miss E. Barrowcliffe. The Princess Royal was then shown around the home that had been converted into a number of wards comprising seventy-five beds in total.

The rooms overlooked the beautiful gardens and terraces, where patients able to walk were free to stroll and enjoy the sunshine. The Princess Royal looked around the billiard room and watched two of the patients engaged in a game of draughts. She then went to the headquarters of the Sheffield Red Cross, where she watched voluntary workers engaged in all kinds of tasks. In the department where clothes were made and sorted, a shawl caught her eye. She was presented with it in order to supply it as a pattern to other workers. Before she left the city to travel to Rotherham, she told the officers that she had seen several things that were new to her and would pass on those new ideas to other organizations.

Her Royal Highness also visited Sheffield to inspect the anti-aircraft gun stations on 22 January 1942. Once again in her official role she saw ATS girls doing a variety of jobs, although none of them was manning the guns. Many of the girls were on 'stick guard', carrying sticks rather than guns. A major later told a local reporter: 'Don't think that it would be simple to get past them [the ATS girls] just because they carry sticks.' He told him that all the girls were trained in ju-jitsu and offered a pretty effective resistance force if it proved necessary. On this occasion, the Princess Royal's inspection was much more thorough than previously and lasted for most of the day. She questioned many of the girls on their welfare and work conditions before looking at the NAAFI hut, which was decorated very brightly and held a stage where the girls put on concerts. Once again the Princess Royal returned to Sheffield in August 1942 when she kept ten engagements in five hours. During her visit, the ATS girls gave demonstrations of putting out fires, treating the injured and eating an 'al fresco' meal prepared by trench cooking.

On 12 January 1940 yet another eminent but more local visitor was the Duke of Norfolk who held several leases in and around the district of Sheffield. He was dressed in the uniform of a major of a southern regiment when he visited the city. The duke was making a tour of the Sheffield Royal Hospitals of which he was president, accompanied by his agent, Mr C.S. Sandford. The two men were shown around the hospital by the matron Miss Sampson and other hospital officials. He was particularly anxious to see the new extension that had been opened by his wife the Duchess of Norfolk just three years earlier. During his visit he spoke to several heroes of the blitz. He was first introduced to Mr Luigi Massara, the restaurant manager of the Grand Hotel, Sheffield who had rescued a man during the height of the air-raids and saved his life. The man in question was Joseph Banks who was with a friend when a bomb fell, injuring him badly. Mr Massara put him onto a door that had been blown off in the raid. With the help of a Scottish soldier, the door carrying Mr Banks was placed on the roof of a car and was held in place there by the two men while he was driven to the Royal Hospital as bombs continued to fall on the city. Once they arrived and he saw that the injured man was safe, the Scottish soldier disappeared and no one knew his name. Mr Massara told the duke that he was British-born of Italian parents and his father had been injured in the last war while fighting for Britain. The duke also spoke to Mr Bernard Norman, an air-raid victim who had lost his wife in the bombings. Mr Norman's 2-year-old child Carol had also been injured and was at that time in the children's hospital in Sheffield. Last of all the duke spoke to Bernard Mitchell, an apprentice electrician who was sheltering in a cellar when his house was hit and his mother was killed. Later the duke went to visit the Estate Office at the Corn Exchange, the Shrewsbury Hospital for elderly people and the Royal Infirmary before taking a motor tour around the city. He had lunch at the City Hall with the mayor and mayoress and they discussed the blitz bombing and how the distressed people of Sheffield had been helped when they found themselves homeless. As he left Sheffield he told a reporter: 'It is wonderful to see how everyone is carrying on again after your terrible experience.'

On 8 April 1941 the Home Secretary and Minister of Home Security Herbert Morrison came to Sheffield. Like other eminent visitors, he wanted to know how Sheffield had coped after the blitz. Accompanied by Mr Jowett, the Solicitor General, he also came to make an inspection of the civil defence services in Sheffield. Mr Morrison told the city authorities and heads of the civil defence services after lunch at the Town Hall that Sheffield had one of the best defence organizations in the country. He admitted that one of his main concerns was for those towns and cities of Britain that had not yet suffered from enemy bombing. As Minister of Home Security he felt that such places experiencing 'quiet periods' left people convinced that 'God was on their side' and were congratulating themselves that things were not so bad. Mr Morrison told the assembled crowd that those places that had not experienced any bombing should have been doing more to prepare for the worst. When the attack on Sheffield came, and it was one of the worst in the country, some very serious lessons had been learned. After every big raid on the towns and cities of Britain, the Ministry of Home Security held an 'inquest' in order that any gaps in civil defence might be exposed. However, Mr Morrison stated that the Sheffield City authorities should be rightly proud of themselves following the devastation of the previous December. He added that every Sheffield man and woman should congratulate themselves on the way they had pulled together after the bombing.

He added that the visit of the king and queen to Sheffield had been a great morale-booster for the people of the city. He stated that the bombing of Buckingham Palace on 13 September 1940 had been 'a most idiotic attack' by the Germans. Instead of instilling alarm in the people, they had seriously miscalculated. The bombing had only endeared their Majesties to the general population of Britain and made their visits to the bombed areas like Sheffield more relevant. Mr Morrison then went on to inspect the civil defence arrangements at a local factory and spoke to the workers through amplifying equipment normally used for playing music. He appealed to the workers to strive to their utmost capacity to strike a blow against Hitler and Mussolini. He stated that every member of the government appreciated the spirit of Sheffield and the enterprise of their City Council. In an interview with a local reporter before he left the city, Herbert Morrison told him:

What I have seen during the day has confirmed the reports I have received that the civil defence organisation was very good indeed. I have been impressed by the keenness of the men and women of the civil defence personnel. Far from having being shaken by the blitz, they had grown stronger in their determination and Sheffield was entitled to pat itself on the back.

Two months later on Thursday, 12 June 1941 the Duke of Kent, the younger brother of the king, visited the city while spending the night as the guest of Lord and Lady Riverdale. It was not the first time that the duke had visited Sheffield as he had been in the city on 29 June 1938 to inspect armaments being made in two of Sheffield's steel works. On the Friday morning he inspected a march past of the ATC made up of 200 boys and twenty officers. After the ceremony the duke walked among the boys and asked them such questions as 'What is your work?', 'Do you like your job?' and 'Are you still at school?' It was reported that for most of the boys the answer to the question 'What would you like to become?' was unequivocally 'To join the RAF as soon as possible.' After the inspection he spent many hours walking around the city and talking to the people and asking them how they had fared during the air-raids. Part of the day was spent at the barrage balloon section where the duke watched members of the WAAF repairing and patching the fabric of the balloons. He spoke to a Miss Rita Ruffell who told him that before the war she had been an actress and had appeared in many London stage productions. He then completed his visit by watching some of the new RAF recruits being trained.

A year later the duke visited Sheffield on 10 June 1942, accompanied by his personal RAF attendant Squadron Leader B.J. Fergusson. Once again he won the affection of the people

The Duke of Kent inspecting a march past in June 1941.

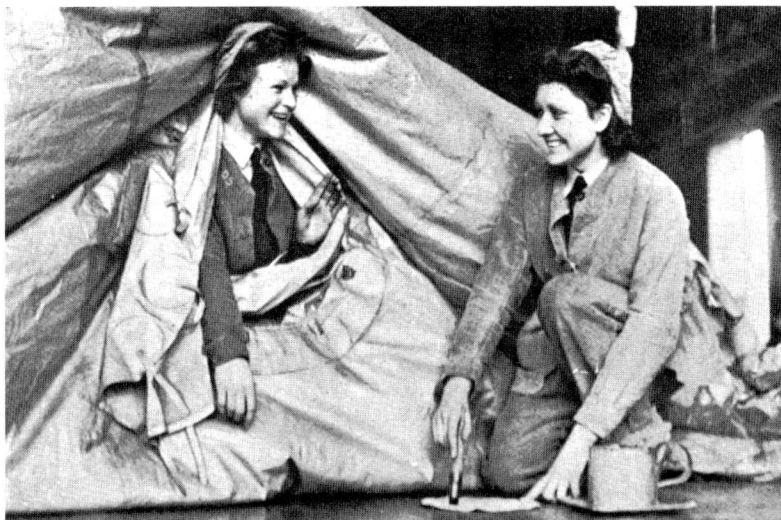

WAAF girls mending barrage balloons.

as he walked over to groups of workmen and began an easy conversation with them. The Home Guard formed a guard of honour and the duke spoke to officers and NCOs in a friendly and approachable manner. Following his introduction to some of the heads of department at the works, the duke was then accompanied to the Sheffield Club where he had his lunch. He then went to the Town Hall where he chatted to about fifty guests specially invited by Lord Mayor Councillor C.J. Mitchell. When it was time for the duke to leave, the crowd was delighted when he took the wheel of the car waiting for him, driving off with Squadron Leader Fergusson. He was cheered by thousands of people who had come to see him off, so it was with great sadness that the people of Sheffield learned only two months later on 25 August 1942 that the duke had been killed in a plane crash while on non-operational duties. His warmth and friendliness to the working men and women of Sheffield had endeared him in their hearts and there is little doubt that they were very sad to hear of his death.

Without exception, the most popular visit to Sheffield was that of Prime Minister Winston Churchill. Although arranged at the very last minute, a large crowd gathered in the centre of Sheffield when it was understood that the PM was making a flying visit to the city on Saturday, 8 November 1941. Mr Churchill was described in one local newspaper as 'the embodiment of British determination.' The PM gave a rousing speech from the balcony of the Town Hall to thousands of people assembled around the vicinity of Pinstone Street in his two and a half hour visit. He told them:

> The British Empire will come through the war united, undaunted, stainless and unflinching. Whilst the British Commonwealth remains united there can be no permanent place in the world for Hitlerism, no corner where it can carry on its brutal doctrine, no hole in which to hide its plotting and planning against the peace of the world.

While speaking of the progress made in the war over the previous two years, the PM stated that the country still needed 'men and women to step into places which are being made for them in the fighting and auxiliary services.' At the conclusion of his speech, Mr Churchill received a gold penknife made of Sheffield steel from the Lord Mayor. The haft bore the Sheffield coat of arms and was engraved with the premier's own signature. He then left to visit two of the city's vital manufacturers where he received an overwhelming ovation. Mr Churchill rode in an open car, seated by the side of the Lord Mayor, and repeated his old trick of holding aloft his hat at the end of his walking stick while prancing police horses provided an escort. The great war leader made another stirring speech at the factory of James Neill and Co. Ltd. As he was entering the factory, he was greeted by the cry of 'Where's thy cigar?' which was quickly rectified when an old soldier commissionaire offered the PM a box of his favourite cigars. As the cavalcade of cars was passing along Castle Street, a young woman from Rotherham called Joan Yarnell impulsively thrust a packet of toffees into the PM's hands. At the entrance gate to the Atlas Works of Messrs Thomas Firth and John Brown Ltd there were even more cheers and waving flags to greet the premier. After visiting several departments and watching the process of a steel furnace being tapped, he was then invited to address the employees from a microphone in the chief office. Mr Churchill told the workers:

I am very proud to come among you today to give you my compliments on the way you are getting on with the work. The work you are doing is playing a vital part in the war. Everyone who keeps his time is doing his bit to rid the world of this curse of war and Hitlerism.

He praised the employees for the fact that only four and a half hours' time had been lost throughout the devastating December air-raids before concluding: 'We have only to hold together to come safely through the dark valley, and then we will see whether we can make something lasting out of our victory.' It was generally thought that the cheers from the people of Sheffield were all the louder because his visit had been so unexpected.

In January 1944 Princess Alice, Duchess of Gloucester, visited Sheffield as she worked closely with the Red Cross. She was travelling through the towns and cities of Britain thanking people for their contributions to the 'Penny a Week' scheme that had been formed to send parcels to British prisoners of war. In November 1939 the Red Cross had established the scheme, asking workers to contribute a penny a week which was deducted from their pay packets. At a time when most people were employed and earning more than £10 a week, it was little hardship. Nevertheless, this fund made an enormous difference to the men of Sheffield who were in prison camps abroad. It was reported that the duchess was wearing a mink coat over a deep purple dress with brown accessories. She told an audience at the Oval Hall that when Sheffield had joined the scheme the sum collected that first month was £148, by September the amount had risen to £1,000 and by December it was £3,662. As a result of these very generous donations, the Red Cross was now sending parcels to 170,000 prisoners including merchant seamen and civilian internees. Each prisoner received a 10lb parcel per week, containing food, tobacco, biscuits and games. The duchess told the audience that board games were particularly popular among the men and several of them had established entertainment groups which had been encouraged by the Germans.

The duchess arrived at the Town Hall where she was greeted by the Lord Mayor before being taken on a visit to see some of the workers who had contributed to the scheme at the Laycock Engineering Company. There she saw many of the machinists at work and spoke enthusiastically to one of the oldest workers who was employed on one of the heavy machines. She was 60-year-old Mrs McWilliams of Cartmell Road, Sheffield, who told her that the other workers called her 'grandma'. In another section the duchess spoke to a Mrs Raley of Wingerworth Avenue, Beauchief who told her that she enjoyed 'setting up' the machines. After her tour of the works, the duchess was told by the managing director Mr W.G. Pallett that the workers had contributed £1,000 a year towards the scheme out of their pay packets. The duchess thanked the workers for their contributions on behalf of the prisoners of war.

The duchess then went to Woodville Leave Hotel, Broomhall where she found some newly-baked cakes being produced in the kitchen by Mrs Kirk, one of the WVS workers, for the servicemen's tea. There she spoke to 'Stephan', a Polish airman who had left Poland four years earlier when he was just 16. She also spoke to two Canadians, Privates Angus Ferrante and Peter McDonald of the RCASC (Royal Canadian Army Service Corps) who had only been in the country for six months and were paying their first visit to Sheffield. The two servicemen told her that they were enjoying their visit, and she told them 'You are very lucky to have such a nice place to stay.' The duchess then visited the Jessop's Hospital for Women where the doctors and nursing staff were lined up to meet her. There she was greeted by the Dower Duchess of Norfolk, Baroness Herries who was president of the hospital. She was shown around the hospital and was particularly interested in five babies that had been born that very morning. Before leaving, the duchess was presented with a bouquet and as she passed along the corridor, there were shouts of 'Three cheers for her.'

These eminent visitors to the city not only brought members of the royal family and the prime minister of Britain to Sheffield, but they also raised the morale of the people. Each of the visitors not only commiserated with the suffering of the people of the city from the savage bombing they had received at the hands of the enemy, but also praised how the city had been reborn after the devastation. Some of them came to learn from the disaster of the blitz, while others like the king and queen just came to show their empathy and support for the people. In all cases they were made to feel very welcome, but perhaps none were initially made more welcome to the city than the American GIs who arrived in 1942 (see Chapter 12). However, they proved to be something of a mixed blessing as they also brought racial problems and eventual resentment from those who claimed they were 'overpaid, oversexed and over here'. Nevertheless, the two nations were united in a tragedy that is still remembered in Sheffield today.

CHAPTER TWELVE

The Americans in Sheffield

Following the bombing of Pearl Harbor in December 1941, the Americans entered the war and for many of these GIs it was the first time they had been out of America. They had heard a lot about England and they took pleasure in coming to visit towns and cities such as Sheffield. In October 1942 two GI sergeants were invited to Sheffield as guests of the *Sheffield Telegraph* newspaper. In an article titled 'Two Yanks Look at Sheffield', it was reported that they were Sergeant Milo Gorton from Yakima, Washington and Sergeant Larry Kears from Coeur d'Alene, Idaho. As they looked around the city they both commented 'Why, this place is really old.' They were impressed by the parquet flooring at the Town Hall and they showed a great interest in the British system of local government as they walked up the alabaster staircase. They admired the Lady Mayoress's beautiful parlour and were amazed to be shown the signature of the king and queen and the Princess Royal in the Visitors' Book. When they too were asked to sign the book, they talked about it for the rest of the day. When they entered the council chamber Sergeant Kears remarked 'Why, this is really good. It's like the Senate; they probably got the idea from England.' The two men then went into the magistrates' courts but were asked to leave when it became clear that the next case was due to be held 'in camera'. However, just a few moments later a police sergeant brought them a message from the bench, inviting them back into the court to hear the case. Afterwards they both remarked that they had been struck by the informality within the courtroom. They said that they liked the way the solicitors talked 'back and forth' to each other and the magistrates, commenting that in the USA all remarks had to be addressed through the bench. Sergeant Gorton was impressed by the blitzed buildings they saw. He said: 'I think it's really funny the way a site is flattened and all the rubble cleared, and then a little sign is put up saying "Business as Usual" down the street.'

The two men later visited High Storrs Grammar School which Sergeant Gorton, as a former teacher, was interested to see. They thought that it looked just like an American high school from the outside and Sergeant Gorton commented that 'We too have plenty of bicycles standing around just like this.' They toured the school, escorted by the head teacher Mr Luther Smith, and were surprised to hear that in many English schools the two sexes were kept separate but they liked the idea of the children wearing school uniforms. Sergeant Kears told a reporter that he had arrived in Sheffield the previous night and found that he could not get accommodation anywhere in the city. Returning to the LMS station, he met a Sheffield man who invited him home for a hot bath and gave him a bed for the night. This unknown man even got up in the morning to make his breakfast and consequently he could not get over the hospitality of the Sheffield people. There is little doubt that the people of the city were friendly towards their American allies but they were also curious as previously they would only have seen them on film, acting as gangsters, cowboys or soldier heroes. When they arrived in the city they brought with them sweets, cigarettes and, most important of all from the female perspective, nylons. Sheffield, which had been on rations for the last few years, took these generous friendly boys to their hearts and they were a great attraction to the ladies.

However, one of the drawbacks to the 'American invasion' was that the GIs also brought segregation to Sheffield. By August 1942 many Sheffielders had never seen a black soldier and they viewed them with much innocent curiosity. On Sunday, 9 August a group of GIs had come to attend a Sunday Fellowship at the Fleur de Lis Centre on Fargate, Sheffield. The next day it was reported that 'Negro Spirituals were the Real Thing' and described how they had been sung in the 'authentic manner'. A 'Negro parson' had been with the men and he spoke of his pleasure at being in Sheffield. The sound of their singing songs such as *Swing Low, Sweet Chariot* and *Down by the Riverside* soared out of the upstairs windows and charmed the people of Fargate as they stopped to listen. One of the sergeants who led the singing told a reporter: 'We are a long way from home. On my journey here, I sometimes regretted it but now I do not.' A month later there was a report of one of the men at the Fleur de Lis, described as a 6ft negro sergeant from New York and weighing over 17 stone, playing popular tunes on the piano before eating his meal of sausage rolls and peas. He told a reporter that he used to play piano in a New York nightclub and told him: 'We have been treated mighty nice. Been enjoying ourselves all the time. We've even been invited out to tea on a Sunday.'

The sergeant was joined by a burly corporal from Greenville, North Carolina and they spoke about the unconscious racism that they had experienced. He related how people in Sheffield used to stare at him in the street and how some white men would get up and walk out of certain premises when he entered. However, they learned to go to places where they were welcome and 'stick to a few places to call.' Two other US army lieutenants told the same reporter that there was little prejudice in Sheffield towards the negroes and added that they had no trouble with the negroes in their charge. One of them added: 'Perhaps it is because they are treated so well, that they feel they must repay people by being on their best behaviour.' By December 1942 Sheffield was playing host to what were described as forty American 'doughboys' who were grateful for being given a meal and a chance to have a wash at the Catholic Women's League House for the Forces on Wilkinson Street, Sheffield. The men had been reported as having travelled a long time as they were unable to park up their lorries which would have caused obstructions in the streets of the bombed-out city. By the time they arrived they were hungry and in need of a welcome break. The men were so grateful that before they left they made a very generous donation to the league.

However welcoming the Sheffield people were to the Americans, they could not take away the boredom of having nothing to do on Sundays. There had been many complaints and applications to open cinemas throughout the war years but all had been rejected by the Watch Committee. The Americans found it particularly irksome as there was little to do with their time off. Cinema proprietors had even offered to make a charitable contribution of up to £1,500 to open on Sundays but this too had been rejected. In September 1942 a

Sheffield Telegraph reporter went on to the streets of the city and asked several people what they could like to see open. Various suggestions were made, from the cinemas to dances. A captain in the United States army agreed that cinemas should be open on Sundays and told the reporter: 'The Sheffield people are grand. Very much more friendly than I had been led to expect, and we are being treated better than at home.' Three negro sergeants were the next to be interviewed and they told him: 'We'd like to go to the films like we can at home, and they should make an effort to make this a home from home for us.'

The influx of Americans in Sheffield by July 1942, many of whom were stationed around the city, was causing some problems. The police and the military authorities seemed to be in some need of clarifying whose responsibility these Allied soldiers were. The chief constable pointed out in the General Order Book that his officers were to ensure that the American soldiers were made to feel at home in this country. He said that the laws of Britain were strange to them and the differences of habit and social outlook made it difficult for newcomers to immediately adapt to our ways. Major James admitted that it was important to bear this in mind and to appreciate that ignorance of the law in such circumstances was excusable. He urged his men to ensure that everything should be done to promote the friendliest relations between the two allies and because of that a great responsibility fell upon the officers of the Sheffield Police Force. For example, he added that many of the Americans were very flash with their money and would handle large 'wads' in front of people who had had very little for many years. Where possible, he urged his men to point this out to our American friends; that it might be thought a little insensitive in wartime circumstances. Even Major James felt it necessary to warn his men that 'as police officers they will come into contact with such men, many of whom are coloured.' He told them that when an American was caught in a flagrant crime, no charges should be made if the military authorities themselves were prepared to deal with the matter. However, he instructed his men to help American soldiers in the city in every possible way. Yet there were circumstances in which the US military took their own action and this resulted in the first court martial being held in Sheffield in December 1943.

The prisoner was Private John William Bolden, described as a 'coloured soldier', who was charged with the manslaughter of Mrs Irene Walton aged 23 of School Road, Sheffield, and another American soldier, Staff Sergeant William Henry Wiggins. He was also charged with injuring Edna Falding of Duke Street, Sheffield and Phyllis Watson of Norris Road, Sheffield. There was a further charge of wrongfully using and damaging a Jeep belonging to the US government. Bolden pleaded not guilty to all charges. The prisoner had been on military police duty at a railway station and was in the process of checking the passengers when he found two girls on the platform who had missed their train to Sheffield. Eventually he agreed to take them to Sheffield and also offered Sergeant Wiggins and another girl a lift. Witnesses said that on the journey he was driving too fast and a heavy fog had obscured the view when all of a sudden a wall appeared before them. Private Bolden pulled the wheel over and the Jeep began to zigzag across the road, eventually turning upside down, trapping Mrs Walton underneath. Sergeant Wiggins was taken to hospital but died from his injuries a few days later. Bolden said in his defence that he had not intended to take the passengers all the way to Sheffield but just to see them on their way. He could hardly remember anything after the crash as he had lost consciousness. However, he admitted that Sergeant Wiggins had asked him for a lift for himself and the girl he was with, even though he knew that civilians were not supposed to be driven in the US army Jeep. His defence argued that the charges of manslaughter be set aside as there was no evidence of recklessness on Bolden's part but the court agreed that the trial was to be continued. Several witnesses gave evidence of Bolden's former good character while he had been in the army and there were no previous convictions on his record. The president of the court announced that the prisoner had been found guilty by the two-thirds majority required in a secret ballot. He was therefore given a dishonourable discharge from the American army, had to forfeit all pay and allowances and be detained in a place determined by the military for a period of two years' hard labour.

Nevertheless, the attraction of these soldiers combined with the GIs' generosity resulted in many Sheffield women throwing themselves at the Americans, to such an extent that the conduct of the American soldiers and their British sweethearts was causing concern to the Sheffield police in July 1944. Chief Constable Mr Lowe reminded his men that they were not judges of morals and he warned them not to intervene in situations except in cases where the law was being breached. He told them:

> One good reason to interfere in such cases was regarding the welfare of the girl. Young girls should have it pointed out to them the dangers they are running by consorting with soldiers of any type. Where applicable the girl's name should be taken and her parents or guardians made aware of the situation. Particular regard should be made to cases of drunkenness or behaviour towards females. Efforts should be made tactfully in the friendliest way to explain to the American soldiers the difference in the customs of the two countries.

There had been many complaints from offended Sheffielders about the troops embracing their girlfriends too openly in public houses, parks and on the main highway. Needless to say, this concern was doubled when young white girls were seen with 'coloured' soldiers. Mr Lowe pointed out that if the girl continued to act inappropriately with the American GIs an order could be obtained under Section 62 of the Children and Young Persons Act 1934 as 'being a person needing care and attention.' Soldiers and girls in such cases should be civilly spoken to and informed that 'Such behaviour is an offence to all decent people in the vicinity.' It should be emphasized that they should not be accused of doing wrong but that their conduct was not a credit either to the uniform or to the female sex. Instead, they should be urged to restrain themselves and avoid giving offence.

Authorization was given to the Sheffield Police the same month that from then on any member of the US army committing offences punishable under laws of the USA should be handed over to the appropriate military authority of the American forces. The subject of Americans carrying arms was discussed as early as 16 December 1942 and as usual the Order Book clarified matters for its officers. It stated that instructions had been given by the US army that arms were only to be carried when required in the performance of a soldier's duty. The carrying of weapons of any kind (apart from small pocket knives with blades of less than 3in) was forbidden. Mr Lowe said:

> If it comes to the attention of any officer that a US soldier is carrying weapons when not on duty, full particulars of the soldier must be obtained. In cases where American servicemen were brought into the police station, they should be immediately handed over to their own military authority for them to deal with the matter.

Nevertheless, he advised his officers who were on the beat to cultivate good working relationships with the military police in order to promote good relations between the British and American authorities.

Relations between the Americans and British in Sheffield were generally pretty good and remained so throughout the war and both countries were united when it became known about the deaths that are inevitable during wartime. In the third week of February 1944, which became known nationally as the 'Big Week', both American and British bombers were united in their determination to smash and destroy German industries. Using intensive bombing raids by the RAF at night and daylight raids by the US Air Force during the day, it was hoped that the combined operations would paralyse industry and demoralize the Germans. On Tuesday, 22 February a massive daylight raid that was intended to demolish a German airfield at Aalborg in occupied Denmark was made. Many of the planes used in these raids were B17s, otherwise known as the 'Flying Fortress' bombers. One of these was named Mi Amigo and was part of 305th Bomb Group. She was part of a twenty-eight-strong group that took off from their base at Chelveston, Northamptonshire at 0800 hours. The crew would have only learned of their mission in a briefing earlier that morning. The men flying Mi Amigo that day were young Americans all aged between 20 and 24. They were all still enthusiastic despite having already flown fourteen missions and consequently were looking forward to flying their fifteenth mission, after which they would be allowed home to the United States for some well-earned R&R.

The pilot was First Lieutenant John Glennon Kriegshauser aged 23 from St Louis, Missouri. He was said to be a quiet man who had a job in a shoe factory before entering the war and was engaged to a girl called Peggy from Ohio. The co-pilot was 2nd Lieutenant Lyle J. Curtis who was a married man also aged 23 from Idaho. He had just recently been informed that his wife Erma was pregnant with the daughter he would never see. The navigator was 2nd Lieutenant John W. Humphrey from Illinois also aged 23. The radio operator was Staff Sergeant Robert E. Mayfield, also from Illinois. Sergeant Charles H. Tuttle aged 21 from Kentucky was the ball turret gunner. In the right waist-gunner position was Sergeant Vito R. Ambrosio aged 24 from Brooklyn, New York who had just been married, having spent only one day with his wife. The left waist-gunner was Master Sergeant George Malcolm Williams aged 23 from Oklahoma who was also a talented guitarist. The bombardier was 2nd Lieutenant Melchor Hernandez from Los Angeles, California, although he had been born in El Paso. He was a very popular man and was an expert at 'jitterbugging' on the dance floor. He was also aged 23 and was the man who had given the name to the aircraft. The flight engineer and top turret gunner was 22-year-old Staff Sergeant Harry W. Estabrooks from Kansas. The tail gunner was the youngest, being only 20 years of age: Staff Sergeant Maurice O. Robbins from Texas who was reputed to be an excellent shot.

The weather was cloudy as the group of B17s was launched and it did not improve by the time they got to the coastline of Denmark. Kriegshauser and the navigator Humphrey knew that the cloud cover was so poor that his crew had little chance of identifying their targets. To make matters worse the squadron was being attacked by flak from 88mm anti-aircraft guns that burst all around them. As they approached, the first wave of German planes came out of the clouds, leaving the squadron little time to fire back. By noon the squadron leader ordered the men to abandon their bombs and head for home. Kriegshauser dropped the 4,000lb bomb they were carrying and turned back to England. Before they had gone very far Mi Amigo was attacked again by a group of Focke-Wulf 190s who were concentrating on the stragglers, of which Mi Amigo was one. Although she managed to escape, it was thought that the plane had lost radio communication and a witness said that the body of the plane was 'in tatters'. Observers noted that more than one of the four engines had failed and the plane appeared to be having difficulty in maintaining altitude. The rest of the squadron returned to their base at Chelveston at full speed, leaving the plane and her ten American airmen to follow as best they could. The squadron leader had given instructions for one of his pilots to try to nurse the badly injured plane back to base, but they lost sight of each other 500 miles off the east coast and after a short search decided that Mi Amigo had gone down in the sea, but in fact the plane did not go down for another four hours.

At some point she went off course and found herself near Sheffield, 100 miles north of the base. It was not clear why she had gone so far off course and it can only be assumed that the navigational equipment had been damaged by the anti-aircraft guns. It was also questioned why the plane was flying at such low altitude. It was deduced that the pilot might have been trying to protect the airmen who were probably subject to intense cold from the damaged fuselage. It was a well-known fact that gunners in their turrets were particularly vulnerable to cold and some literally froze to the fabric of the plane. It may also have been the damage to the plane's engines that resulted in the pilot not having the power to climb to a higher altitude. The cloud cover was down to 500ft and it was again thought that being an experienced pilot, Kriegshauser was hoping to get as far inland as possible in the hope that the cloud would clear, enabling him to take note of his actual position. It was at first thought that the crew were heading for Doncaster, where planes could be landed safely at either of the two air bases of RAF Finningley or RAF Lindholme. However, the weather never improved and it was about 5 pm when the plane found itself over Sheffield. It was later reported that people in Endcliffe Park heard the plane long before it was visible. One story goes that children were playing football in the park and that by this time Kriegshauser was desperately trying to land but on seeing the children he pulled up the nose of the plane and hit the hillside instead. There were differing reports from eye witnesses as to exactly how the plane crashed. Some put it down to engine failure as it was heard to be 'stuttering', while others claimed that the plane hit the trees. Yet more witnesses stated that when the plane hit the ground and came to a halt among the trees, the fuselage was intact. People ran towards the plane and there is a report of one dead body being thrown from the wreckage, although which of the crew it was, there is no evidence. What actually happened was that within minutes a fire broke out inside the plane and it exploded. Although desperate measures were taken to try to rescue the ten-man crew, there was little that could be done. The fire immediately took hold and lasted for hours after the crash.

One of the first men on the scene was Flight Sergeant Clem Payne of Ecclesall Road, Sheffield, who was home on leave at the time and had seen the plane out of the window of his home. He told a *Sheffield Star* reporter that the plane was flying so low that it was possible to see the faces of the crew. He said that as far as he could tell, from the angle at which the plane was flying, it was about to crash. When he reached the scene he found all the crew were dead and with the help of another man he managed to drag the body of the rear gunner out of the fuselage, although he could already see that the man had died. When the fire died down, not surprisingly all the bodies were either badly mutilated or charred. It was suspected that the men who were not already dead when the plane crashed would have died instantly in the explosion. The NFS from Sharrow Vale worked all night to get the fire under control and the remains of the crew out of the plane. Section Officer Cooper said that they saw the plane descending and could see that it was in trouble, and as a consequence his men were already in the tender when they witnessed the explosion.

Trees had been uprooted and crushed under the plane and it was only by mere chance that children playing in the park had not been injured. The plane crashed into the trees behind a refreshment bar and part of the rear wing was torn away by one of the trees. Mr Will Griffiths of Stainton Road, Sheffield didn't actually see the crash but his wife did. When she told him, he ran outside in his slippers and waded across some water to be the second man to reach the plane. The front of it was ablaze and the heat drove them back. He told the firemen that lying on the ground was one body that they pulled away from the plane, although they too could see that the airman was already dead. Another man, Arthur Haynes, was a decorator working on a house near the crash site. He too ran towards the explosion, still wearing his white coat, and he grabbed a hatchet on the way. With the aid of this weapon, some of the men managed to make a hole in the rear of the plane in order to extract the live ammunition before it exploded. Another rescuer who saw the plane crash was postman Mr William McNerlen of Stone Grove, Broomhill, Sheffield. He told rescuers that he was delivering letters when he clearly saw the plane plummet to the earth. It spiralled down before rolling over three times before crashing. He too, having first-aid experience, ran to help.

Another witness was Mrs A.D.H. Clarke who was feeding her hens at the back of her house on Endcliffe Crescent when she heard the plane's engines. In the spirit of the war, she waved to the men in the plane as was her habit, and when she saw the plane turn over she took it for a victory roll. Then she noticed that the plane had descended even lower and gave three more terrific spins before plunging earthwards. The plane skimmed over the top of Endcliffe Grange and she no longer saw it as it disappeared over a garden wall. A second later she heard a terrible crash and flames blazing up into the air and she immediately ran inside to ring the police and the NFS. Another witness was a man called Brian Jackson who was standing in Manchester Road, Sheffield when he saw the crash and he too ran to help. He said 'The plane was jammed vertically upright between two trees and the wings and fuselage were more or less intact', although the forward section was blazing fiercely when he arrived at the scene.

When the tender belonging to the NFS appeared, the men ordered the civilians to leave the area. A cordon of soldiers was hastily erected to keep onlookers away as at that stage it was unclear whether any live bombs were on board. The NFS firemen extracted water from a brook to try to extinguish the flames and foam was also used. The next day the creamy foam was still visible on the pathways. Steel-helmeted NFS men, civil defence workers, soldiers and ambulance men were all at the scene within minutes. When the fire died down, ropes were put around the wings and they were pulled away in order to free the inside of the aircraft to bring the rest of the bodies out. Over an hour after the crash, flames could clearly be seen licking at the wreckage. Four hours later the rescuers were still attempting to clear the crash site, working by the light of acetylene flares.

One of the rescuers was a man called Jim Hodgson who told a *Star* reporter in February 2014 about the plane crash. He stated that it was only the heroic actions of the pilot who avoided homes in Greystones and the children playing in the park that ensured there were no deaths of people on the ground. Mr Hodgson was a Hillsborough highway worker who had been trained in rescuing bodies from wreckage and he went to the aid of the other rescuers. For his actions in trying to crash the plane as far away from the children and the houses as possible, the US Air Force awarded the pilot a posthumous DFC for minimizing the loss of life. Their historical records state that Lieutenant John Kriegshauser 'displayed consummate skills as he piloted the aircraft back to England although unfavourable weather conditions were prevalent.' At the time of the crash it was presumed that the pilot was trying to find a field in which to land but it was supposed that the damaged engines became unresponsive over the city of Sheffield. The report continued: 'It crashed into a wood approximately 100 yards away from the houses. The courage, coolness and skill displayed by Lt. Kriegshauser reflect the high credit on himself and the Armed Forces of the US.'

It has been estimated that on that same night as many as forty-three American bombers were lost, with crews totalling 430 men. Among them were Mi Amigo and another plane that also never made it back to base. All the crew were originally buried in an American military cemetery in Cambridge, but after the war the remains of Kriegshauser, Curtis, Humphreys, Hernandez, Mayfield, Ambrosio and Williams were returned to the United States for reburial.

Sheffield has never forgotten the bravery of the crew, and a legacy of that is that since 1970 a memorial service has been held at the site by the Sheffield branch of the Royal Air Force Association. To permanently remember the men, two plaques were also installed that same year, funded by donations from the people of Sheffield. One of the memorial stones reads:

ERECTED BY
SHEFFIELD R.A.F. ASSOCIATION
IN MEMORY OF
THE TEN CREW OF U.S.A.A.F. BOMBER
WHICH CRASHED IN THIS PARK
22.2.1944
PER ARDUA AD ASTRA

There is another plaque with the names of all the crew inscribed on it. Wreaths from the US Air Force and the RAF are laid on a Sunday every year, as near as possible to the date when the plane crashed.

Throughout the war years there were other plane crashes in and around the city of Sheffield. On 26 January 1941 a Blenheim Bomber crashed and three of the crew were killed. Three months later on 19 April a Hampden Bomber crashed in Concord Park, killing one of the crew and leaving the others injured. The following year on 17 July 1942 three out of a crew of five were injured when a Wellington Bomber crashed on the Hallam Moors. Nevertheless, it was the end of Mi Amigo that stayed in the hearts of Sheffield people for many years. To further honour the crew, a grove of ten American oaks, one for each crew member, was planted in 1969. Also a No. 10 Sheffield bus was christened 'Mi Amigo' in honour of the American airmen who died at Sheffield in 1944.

The two plaques commemorating the crash of Mi Amigo and the names of the crew.

CHAPTER THIRTEEN

Peace at Last

By Christmas of 1944 it finally seemed that peace was in sight. Slowly but surely, families were being reunited with their loved ones as the men began to return home. One lucky naval officer who was home on leave that Christmas went along to his son's party held at the Denby Street Nursery School. Little Billy Gillott told the staff that 'Daddy is my Christmas present. He came last night when I was in bed.' There was plenty of food at the party that some of the children hadn't seen for many years, such as cakes, jellies, blancmange, fruit and mince pies. Another reunited family was that of Rifleman Albert Uttley who was interviewed while carving the Sunday joint at his home on Dunlop Street, Sheffield in January 1945. He had been away from home for two and a half years and his son, now aged 3, could hardly contain his excitement at having his daddy back.

Men returning home on leave from the war started appearing in the city that January and there had been strong criticism that when they got to the station in the early hours there was no transport to get these heroes to their homes. As a consequence the men were left to walk, sometimes for many miles, to the outskirts of the city. There was great indignation in the early hours of Tuesday, 2 January 1945 when men who had served in the D-Day landings found themselves having to walk home. Mr H. Watson of the Sheffield Transport Department claimed he had not had the information that the servicemen would be arriving and that subsequently no transport had been arranged for them. Among the men was Leading Aircraftman Alan Morton of Peveril Road, Sheffield who had been travelling non-stop for forty-three hours, including a motor lorry journey on the Continent. The following week there were more complaints from servicemen who arrived at the station at 3 am from Burma, yet again to find there was no organized transport. As one of them said to a reporter who met the train: 'They might as well call us the forgotten army.' Another stated that he had travelled with a party of thirty Sheffield and district men who had served in the Far East and who had not seen their homes for years. They arrived at the station cold, tired, hungry and laden with equipment. A reporter had met the train and seen for himself how tired the travellers were. Following a telephone call from the same reporter, a duty truck was sent out by the railway company which took some men to their homes in Sheffield, the rest having already departed.

However, the Sheffield authorities were quick to amend the situation and by 17 January a reporter was informed of the 'Get You Home Scheme' that would soon be in operation. This would ensure that all soldiers arriving in the early hours would be carried to the inner suburbs by a Corporation Inner Circle bus. Those who lived further out of the city would find other private transport waiting for them. The scheme had been organized by Major B.P. Hall, an Army Welfare officer who told a reporter that he had asked for volunteer car owners who wished to drive the men home to apply to some new offices just opened at Spooner Road, Broomhill, Sheffield. Petrol coupons would be available to those holding a permit for the scheme. Thankfully, after this rocky start, those soldiers reaching Sheffield in the early hours were assured of a lift home as more and more drivers volunteered to look after these returning heroes.

Several schemes had been put into operation in Sheffield at the beginning of 1945 to ease the men back to the city of their birth, and one such scheme featured the 'Calling Blighty' recordings from different parts of the Empire. It was reported on 17 January that the Palace Cinema in Union Street, Sheffield showed a scene resembling a café somewhere in India. There was soft music playing extracts from the *Desert Song* in the background and men wearing tropical kit could be seen sitting at a table. The man in the foreground, Sergeant John Crapper who had been overseas for three years, put down his paper and said: 'Hello Sheffield. Greetings to you from all the Sheffield lads in India.' The rest was drowned out by people in the theatre clapping and cheering. Mr and Mrs J. Crapper, the sergeant's parents, were in the crowd, as was his fiancée Miss Gladys Wade who heard him say 'Give my love to Gladys.' Other messages were given to wives, mothers, fathers, aunts and cousins, and even family pets were not left out. Mrs G. Eason received a special message from her son Stewart and the audience cheered each and every one. The people could see for themselves how happy their serving men were as they urged their relatives in Sheffield not to forget to write. Other similar programmes from all parts of the Empire were broadcast on the radio as the men from Sheffield sent warm messages home to the families that they hoped to see soon.

By the summer of 1944 the people of Sheffield could see that the end of the war was in sight as slowly but surely sections of the civil defence teams were closed down. On Monday, 11 September 1944 the men and women of the Fire Guards met for their last duty at the Town Hall, Sheffield. They were fire-watchers who throughout the war had been employed to watch out for incendiary bombs falling on industrial buildings and to prevent small fires from engulfing them. They were often employed throughout the night and it was a very onerous and boring job. It appears that the anthem *Jesus Shall Reign Where'er the Sun* had been sung by Fire Guard Tom Clarke from the top of the Town Hall in 1941, and since that time it had become a tradition. A recording of the hymn had been played every night since, before their duty began. The last supper party was something of a celebration and the chair of the Emergency Committee thanked every Fire Guard in the city as he told them: 'I feel that the spirit of service will not go when the war is over, but that a better public spirit will exist than ever before in the history of the country.'

The reporter stated that at the celebration the atmosphere was upbeat as the men and women forgot their grumbles, their lost sleep, their warm beds at home and just reminisced about the good times they had had. There was no sentiment; the feeling in the room was just that the Fire Guards were glad to be rid of an irksome duty. Chief Warden Captain Roberts stated that although fire-watching would be slowly ended, the machinery would still be maintained and that Fire Guard captains and leaders should be prepared to bring their present arrangements into operation at a moment's notice, should the need arise.

One would have thought that most of the people of Sheffield would be glad to see the back of the blackout, but curiously some were reluctant to let go of it. At a time when most public houses and shops were now lit up as they had been in pre-war days, most of the smaller houses in the city declined to light up completely. On 15 April 1944 along Moore Street, Sheffield, there were only three houses lit of around 100 houses in the street. One of the residents, Mrs Joan Skidmore, told a reporter: 'I think they ought to keep the lights switched off until the war is definitely over.' A neighbour who lived close by agreed, admitting that she was still frightened that there might be a repeat of the bombing as she closed her shutters for the night. Across the road Mr and Mrs J.W. Wentworth were having a cigarette while a light showed through their pretty amber curtains. Mr Wentworth said, however, that they were not intending to leave the light on, 'they just wanted to see what it looked like.'

When news came to Sheffield that men of a light anti-aircraft regiment were arriving the next day on 20 April 1945 the station rapidly filled up with relatives and family members. There was quite a crowd to greet the train carrying many servicemen travelling from Italy whose families had not seen them for four and a half years. One of them was Sergeant Douglas Sanderson, a former Post Office employee of Southey Green Road, Sheffield. He was met by his wife, his son Michael aged 7 and his little daughter Valerie who would be 4 in July. Little fair-haired Valerie did nothing but cry as she hid behind her mother's legs, eying the father she had never met before. Sergeant Sanderson, who won his MM in the desert, told his wife: 'I think she is beautiful.' The platform was crowded as men greeted their wives, girlfriends and parents. Bombardier M.D. Perrett even carried a Spanish guitar that he had bought from an Italian. Throughout the city these men continued to return home to the city of their birth, greeted by their families and no doubt thankful that they had survived, while still remembering those comrades that hadn't.

There was a spirit of optimism in Sheffield that had been missing from the people over the last five years as they looked on the future with some hope at last. On 2 May 1945 Sheffield was preparing for the victory celebrations when it was announced that the air-raid warning system that had alerted the city on 130 occasions was to be abolished at midday. There were great celebrations at this news as people realized that the war really was coming to an end and finally they could celebrate the peace. Plans were put in place and the local newspapers reported what was going to happen. It was announced that two hours after Winston Churchill announced the end of the war in Europe, a service would be held at the Sheffield City War Memorial in Barker's Pool. There was to be a two-minute silence, the same as that held during the Armistice Day service. The Town Hall would be floodlit and searchlights would be mounted on the roof of the City Hall. Flags of all nations were ready to decorate the Town Hall, where there were to be ten 'V' signs in red, white and blue lights erected on the building. Four would be on the clock tower, one on the Cheney Row side, one over the main entrance in Pinstone Street and four on the Surrey Street side. The largest would be on Cheney Row which would be 21ft high and visible for a great distance along the Moor.

So it was with some tension that people waited outside Sheffield Town Hall on the night of Monday, 7 May 1945 waiting for the news that the VE celebrations would be held the following day. Men and women wearing buttonholes of any object, just so long as it was red, white and blue, leaned

Sheffield Town Hall where thousands waited on the night of Monday, 7 May 1945 to hear about the next day's VE-Day celebrations.

against the railing waiting for the news. Many had come into the city centre ready to rejoice and a delay in the declaration left them feeling lost and disappointed. Others doubted that peace really had come and were just waiting for confirmation before the celebrations could really begin. Nevertheless, public houses were doing a thriving trade as people were preparing to enjoy themselves, declaration of peace or not. The city was filled with pictures of the Allied leaders erected on the sides of large buildings amid their national colours. Flags of the United Nations and the British Dominions were everywhere to be seen. In the factories and workshops employees also decorated the buildings, although there was one grim note at the premises of Thomas Firth and John Brown Ltd. It was reported that an effigy of Hitler along with a paintbrush and swastika hung over one of the machines. Sheffield Transport Department had illuminated trams ready to go into service to cover all the main routes. Finally at 7 pm the announcement came that the whole country would have two days' holiday to celebrate the end of the war. The prime minister told the people of Britain:

This is your victory... In all our long history we have never seen a greater day than this. Everyone, man or woman, has done their best. Everyone has tried. Neither the long years, nor the dangers, nor the fierce attacks of the enemy have in any way weakened the independent resolve of the British nation. God bless you all.

When the speech was finished the people of Sheffield cheered and sang. The centre of the city became a huge dance floor as the illuminated Town Hall clock pointed to one minute past midnight. Thousands made the High Street impassable and the square in front of the Town Hall was solid with jubilant cheering crowds. Barker's Pool and Pinstone Street became an orgy of conga lines and rumbas. Trams making their way around the crowded city centre were forced to ring their bells to ward off the seemingly endless lines of people, arms linked and singing songs of victory. The song *Roll Out The Barrel* was the most popular. From the suburbs came the glow of bonfires that were kept burning long into the early hours. Floodlights shone on the

Barker's Pool, which was packed with dancers, conga lines and jubilant crowds.

civic buildings and people seemed stunned by a brilliance they had not seen since pre-war days.

Outside the city centre, the rejoicing was the same. It was reported that a Mrs Crookes of Parkwood Road, Sheffield listened to the PM's speech and as soon as his words had died away, that was the signal for the bonfires to be lit. Taking a box of matches she went across to light two gigantic bonfires that had been built on waste land opposite her house. Children who had also been listening to the premier's speech ran out of their houses to watch the lighting of the bonfires. A neighbour had strung up an effigy of Hitler and placed it on top of one of the bonfires. The children cheered loudly as the fires, the like of which they had not seen in years, were lit. In Farfield Road, Sheffield neighbours had also arranged a bonfire around which a huge sack of potatoes was being baked for the children. Someone had managed to get hold of some fireworks and they were lit for children who had never seen fireworks before in their lives. As dusk fell, doors and windows were flung open and wirelesses turned up to full pitch for street dancing. A tree in Burnside Avenue was decorated with lights and elsewhere the streets held children's races as people celebrated. There were literally miles of bunting to be seen in the streets and 'V' signs were painted everywhere.

Two hours later crowds gathered, pressing against the barriers on Pinstone Street to wait for the official celebrations to begin. As the crowds waited they sang and laughed. A woman in a red, white and blue dress climbed on top of the closed gates of the Town Hall and conducted the singing of *Land of Hope and Glory*. This was followed by *It's a Long Way to Tipperary* and *Pack Up Your Troubles*. Finally the Lord Mayor and Lady Mayoress, Councillor and Mrs C.G. Marlow proceeded towards Barker's Pool memorial for the dead, where a service of remembrance was held. The service was described as being simple, dignified and impressive. A two-minute silence was held, during which many of the crowd appeared to be weeping, before the silence was broken by the *Last Post* being played by the boys of the Sheffield Sea Cadet Corps. As the local newspaper stated: 'Sheffield VE-day rejoicings were tempered by acts of humble reverence and heartfelt thanksgiving for mercies vouchsafed with remembrance of those whose sacrifice helped to make victory possible.'

The Lord Mayor, after appealing for unslackened endeavour until the war in the Far East was won, recalled the early days of the war when young men and women were called to fight to defend 'our island home'. Radio speakers transmitted the half-hour service, prayers and hymns across the city.

The War Memorial at Barker's Pool where a Service of Remembrance was held on Tuesday, 8 May 1945. Note shrapnel damage still on base.

The following day on Tuesday, 8 May the VE celebrations began in earnest. Although it had been designated as a holiday, because of the earlier confusion as to whether the celebrations would start or not, many people turned up for work only to be sent home again. Despite the general feeling of happiness, the weather was poor and there was a downpour after lunch that kept most people indoors. The day seemed to be a mixture of emotions and sentiments for all: the old, the middle-aged and the young. Hourly services, lasting for fifteen to twenty minutes each, were held in the cathedral starting at 9 am the following day. They were to continue until the King's Speech at 9 pm. There were queues at the cathedral for the hourly services, many standing in line before the last service had finished. Later it was estimated that between 16,000 and 18,000 people had attended throughout the day. All walks of life were represented in these services: housewives with their shopping bags, parents with their children, servicemen and women, business people and workers. The Bishop of Sheffield Dr L.S. Hunter told a reporter: 'This Cathedral has been simply swamped with people today. It seems as though the great heart of Sheffield turned instinctively to its old Parish Church to express its thanksgiving to Almighty God for the tremendous victory we celebrate today.'

Those that had lost relatives and friends in the conflict were not forgotten. Reverend William Wallace of the Sheffield Methodist Church gave a service for the bereaved at the Victoria Hall in the afternoon. There was also one place in Sheffield that did not celebrate VE day and where there were no flags and people stayed indoors all day. They were the forlorn and defeated Germans at the prisoner of war camp at Lodge Moor. They seemed bewildered and could not believe the news, which they thought was impossible. However, the noise and cheering from the people of the city was heard in the camp and they had to accept the truth of it when they saw a huge 'V' erected on the side of Lodge Moor Hospital.

At 9 pm the King's Speech was described as being 'one of the most impressive Sheffield scenes, when about 30,000 people gathered at the Town Hall to hear it.' Trams came to a standstill from the High Street and Fargate on one side and the Moor head on the other. The crowd stood in respectful silence as the speech was relayed through loudspeakers from the Town Hall. The king told them:

> Today we give thanks to Almighty God for our great deliverance. Speaking from our Empire's oldest capital city, war-battered but never for one moment daunted or dismayed, I ask you to join with me in that act of thanksgiving... Armed or unarmed, men and women, you have fought and striven and endured to your utmost. No one knows that better than I do, and as your King I thank with a full heart those who bore arms so valiantly on land and sea, or in the air, and all civilians who, shouldering their many burdens, have carried them unflinchingly without complaint.

Remembering people who had made the supreme sacrifice, the king referred to 'those who will not come back, who have laid down their lives.' There was complete silence until His Majesty's speech was finished, when the crowd erupted in loud cheers before breaking into a simultaneous rendition of the National Anthem. Following the speech, there were more celebrations and the sound of singing could be heard long into the evening. Over the following day the merriment continued with street parties, impromptu dances and lines of conga-dancing in the city centre. It was said that even on Thursday, 10 May: 'The city still rang with the merriment of children and the midnight jubilation of thousands of adults. Sheffield breweries worked on both VE holidays and as a result less than 5 per cent of the public houses sold out of beer.'

On Sunday, 13 May services of thanksgiving were led by the different denominations of the city. The morning service at the cathedral was of a civic nature, whereas the afternoon open-air service in Weston Park took the form of a military parade. The service was led by the Bishop of Sheffield accompanied by Reverend William Wallace. The bishop, in his address, praised God for deliverance and honoured the splendid sacrifice of the men and women of Sheffield. Reverend Wallace reminded people that victory was an opportunity to start building a better Britain. Despite the rain, people in their thousands gathered in Weston Park to watch the parade that went along the route to

Weston Park, where a military parade was held on Sunday, 13 May 1945.

the Town Hall, along Western Bank, Hounsfield Road, Glossop Road, Division Street, Cambridge Street and Pinstone Street. The parade, led by Colonel Neill, comprised nearly 5,000 members of all the civil defence services of the city. There were thirteen bands leading the 2-mile-long parade which took half an hour to pass the Town Hall where the mayor took the salute. The march included members of the Home Guard, airborne troops, Royal Engineers, RASC, RAF, WAAF, British Red Cross and St John's Ambulance. Perhaps the loudest cheers were kept for the members of the 'Old Contemptibles' of British Legion veterans.

On Sunday, 3 June 1945 another 'stand-down' parade was held for the civil defence services as Sheffield said 'thank you' to the thousands of men and women who had defended the city over the past six years. Heavy rain fell as the first part of the parade moved off from Exchange Street to the Town Hall, where the salute was taken by Sir William Bartholomew, the North-East Regional Commissioner. The parade was made up of wardens, ambulance, first-aid rescue, messengers, Fire Guards, shelter marshals and rest centre staff. The second part of the ceremony was held in the City Hall where the Lord Mayor introduced one of their number who had defied the weather. He was 80-year-old warden W.J. Robinson of Pitsmoor who rose to his feet as cheers and applause filled the hall. The mayor told the people: 'Sheffield is proud of you. The many acts of heroism you performed, men and women alike, in December 1940 will long stand out in the annals of our city.' Sir William Bartholomew said that 'speaking as a servant of the state for many years he had never met more forthrightness, co-operation and initiative than Sheffield had shown to him.'

At the final stand-down dinner of the ARP service held in July 1945, Captain Roberts paid tribute to the staff of the many firms in the city. He told them that 'by their bravery and resource they had contributed to one of Britain's greatest triumphs.' The dinner that was given by the directors of the *Sheffield Star* and *Sheffield Telegraph* was held at Kemsley House when Captain Roberts made a toast to 'Sheffield's ARP service'. He told them:

> Unlike the armed forces, the civil defence of the city started out entirely without precedent. By trial and error and the spirit of determination and sacrifice the service made such a difference that was not realised at the time. Individual firms had played a great part, and the city owes them a great debt of gratitude.

He concluded that he wished he could have given the service a more fitting 'burial' and if it had been left to him he would have held a National Civil Defence Day as their efforts had been worth more than just a casual stand-down.

Even though the civil defence teams were being stood down, the war with Japan continued. Sheffield people, along with the rest of Britain, longed for a complete end to all hostilities, which only came when Japan surrendered on the afternoon of 15 August 1945. New Prime Minister Clement Atlee confirmed the news at midnight, saying that 'the last of our enemies is laid low.' Despite the late hour, the rejoicing in Sheffield began immediately as the city leaped back into life. Bonfires were lit, fireworks and rockets were launched and cheering and shouting began in every corner of the city. Thousands of people went again to Barker's Pool to attend another commemoration service that should have taken place two hours after the announcement had been made. However, when it became known that the service would now take place the following day, people remained to dance and sing for hours. The song most sung was *Lilli Marlene* that could still be heard at 2 am 'underneath the lamplight' at Barker's Pool. Many people, disturbed from their sleep, walked the street still in their nightwear as children stoked the fires, watching the coloured lights which even at that late hour once again bloomed around the city. A jazz band started to play and yet another giant conga line started as people danced through the streets of Neepsend and Hillfoot Bridge. Visiting street by street, the line swelled until at one point it was estimated to be made up of almost 8,000 people.

The illuminated 'V' signs and clock towers were once again turned on and they lit up the streets. Crowds in Queens Road, Sheffield were dancing around a piano that had been dragged from one of the houses into the middle of the road. The hilarity did not die down until the middle of the night and fires were still glowing at dawn. One group of boys could be spotted using the introduction 'Excuse me, it's "V" night' to kiss every pretty girl within an easy radius. Navigating any street in the city centre was fraught with difficulties from exploding fireworks to avoiding palais gliding parties. There were paddlers in the fountains of the Town Hall gardens and the loneliest man in the city was reported to be the police constable on duty there. Surrounded by thousands of people, he just looked benignly on things that didn't quite conform to normal behaviour.

The following day, which had officially been designated Victory Day, started with the ringing of the bells across Sheffield to mark the final end of hostilities. Stunned civilians, the very few who had slept through the night's excitement, awoke to the news and a day of organized festivities. They began early as the city authorities put into effect plans that had been ready 'just in case'. Six of the parks – Millhouses, Endcliffe, Concord, Hillsborough, High Hazel and Longley – had dancing to bands and concert parties organized. Many people went to church, while others joined long queues for food for their families. From lunchtime the public houses were full and many had to queue to get inside for a drink. The commemoration service at Barker's Pool was held at midday, with the Lord Mayor telling his people:

> A great price has had to be paid to achieve this success. At this time in the hour of our rejoicing, let us pause to remember those whose hearts are sad at the loss of dear ones. Difficult times are ahead if we are to make our city and country worthy of the sacrifices made, the way will be hard and there will be plenty for all to do.

Once again there were fourteen thanksgiving services held at the cathedral that were very well attended. In between the services the bell-ringers were kept busy with victory peals during the thirty-minute intervals. Dancing continued as the City Hall broadcast dance music, although scarcely a note was heard over the shouts and cheers. Bonfires glowed everywhere, and from the early hours the main streets of the city became choked. Human chains made up of scores of young people wound their way through the streets, clinging onto the waist of the person in front of them. Cruising cars loaded with people who had come into the city centre were greeted by men and boys jumping onto the running boards and bumpers. Children were carried by their parents watching the events with complete astonishment from the safety of parental arms.

At 9 pm the king made his broadcast to the nation from his study at Buckingham Palace and once again his words were relayed from loudspeakers fixed at the City Hall. He said that three months had passed since they celebrated the end of the war with Germany:

> We then rejoiced that peace had returned to Europe, but we knew that a strong and relentless enemy still remained to be conquered in Asia. None of us could then tell how long or how heavy would prove the struggle that still awaited us. Japan has surrendered, so let us join in thanking Almighty God that the war has ended throughout the world, and that in every country men may now turn their industry, skill and science to repairing its frightful devastation, and to building prosperity and happiness.

The Lord Mayor set light to the first rocket to be fired at Endcliffe Park at 9.30 pm and shortly afterwards bonfires and fireworks could be seen in three other Sheffield parks.

As Sheffield celebrated the end of the hostilities, the people looked forward to living in peace for the future. Undoubtedly there were problems; men coming home from the war and having to become fathers again, settling in to what would probably seem to be a humdrum life once more. Women, who for many years had made their own decisions and had their freedom, would now be forced to return to being just housewives and homemakers again. Today, new shops and businesses have been built over the ruins left by the blitz and the extensive redevelopment still continues.

The story of Sheffield during the war years is one of men and women acting with great courage and fortitude to help others. Members of the Emergency Committee, the Home Guard and other civil defence workers had worked together tirelessly to protect the people of the city. They showed through their courage and determination a spirit of defiance against oppression as they responded wholeheartedly to the call to action. Our world today is a better place because of them.

Sources

Sheffield Archives	Reference Number
Air Raid Precaution Minutes	CA-ARP 2/1 & 2
Home Office Coroners' Reports	934-511
ARP Damage Report	CA538 (4) (5)
ARP Circular	2010/146
Emergency Civil Defence Minutes and Reports	CA-EMG/1/7
Diary of Mrs Gloria Hallett	MD6795/1
Diary of Ruth Atkin	2013/21
Letter from Eliza Kate Askew	MD7581
SY Police General Order Book	SY295/C1/10

Book Sources

Sheffield Telegraph and Star Ltd, *Sheffield at War 1939–1945*, (1948)

Charles Simms JP, *Charlie's War: Memoirs of a Linseed Lancer*, Grosvenor House Publishing Ltd, (2012)

Newspaper Sources

Sheffield Star
Sheffield Telegraph
The Times
Sheffield Telegraph and Independent

Electronic Sources

Mi Amigo: The Fate of a Flying Fortress http://h2g2.com/approved_entry/A7563783

Courage Above the Clouds by Paul Allonby (eBook published on kindle) 2014

http://www.sfbhistory.org.uk/downloads/CourageAboveThe Clouds.pdf

Index

Abbeydale Grammar School, 29
Adam, Lt Gen Sir Ronald, 41
Alexander, Dr W.P., 28–9
Alfred Road, 114
Algus, Mr B., 91
Anderson Shelters, 5, 17, 38, 58,
    60, 62, 91, 158
Arthur Balfour, 17
Asbury, Cllr W., 2–4, 9–10, 42, 84,
    89
Askew, Eliza K., 62–4
Ashmore, E., 44
Aspinall, Alfred, 60
Aston Street, 114
Atkin, Ruth, 65–6, 69
Attercliffe Road, 43

Baker, Mrs Edward, 115–16
Balm Green, 51
Baines, Henry, 104
Banks, Joseph, 162
Banks, Sally, 112
Barkers Pool, 9, 51, 126, 187–8,
    190, 194–6
Barnsley Road, 87
Bartholomew, Maj Gen Sir
    William, 48, 193–4
Barrowcliffe, E., 160
Bawtry Road, 65
Beaumont, Cyril, 94
Beck, George, 83
Beever, Elsie, 99
Billam, Roy, 74–5
Blackbrook Road, Fulwood, 58
Bolden, Sgt J.W., 174
Bolland, Annie, 111
Boyce, Enid, 31
Branson, Col D.S., 39
Brett Street, 64
Bridge Street, 106

Broadbent, Mrs E., 105
Brown Bayley's Steelworks, 11, 52
Brown, W.H., 73
Burden, Sgt J.T., 44
Burnside Avenue, 189

Cambridge Street, 193
Carlisle Street East, 129
Cartmell Road, 168
Castle Street, 51, 121
Castleton, Dorothy, 116
Cathedral, 10, 51, 55, 126, 191
Cedar Lane, 110
Central Library, 144
Central Picture House, 72–4
Chambers, Elsie, 156
Charlotte Road, 54
Cheney Row, 187
Chippinghouse Lane, 104
Churchill, Winston, 166–7, 187
City Hall, 6, 101, 147, 153, 162,
    193, 196
City General Hospital, 34
City Road, 52
Clarke, Fire Guard Tom, 185
Clarke, Mrs A.D.H., 180
Clements, Vincent, 156
Coggan, Sarah Ann, 130–1
Coleford Road, 85, 157
Coleridge Road, Attercliffe, 83
College of Arts and Crafts, 29
Collie, Mr J.M., 53
Colquhoun, J.F., 21
Colver, Cllr R., 22
Concord Park, 69, 182, 195
Cookswood Road, 61
Cooper, Fred, 98
Cooper, Robert Horace, 157
Cooper, Section Officer, 179
Coronation Street, 110

Crapper, Sgt John, 184
Crapper, Mr and Mrs J., 184
Crofts, Leslie, 83–4
Crookes, Audrey, 30–1
Crookes, Avril, 30–1
Crookes Cemetery, 83
Crookes, Mrs, 189
Currie, Leslie Harold, 75–7

Dansmere Road, Pitsmoor, 99
Davies, Alice, 124–5
Davies, W.G., 93
Dawson, Harry, 52
Dawson, Maisie, 116
Denby Street Nursery School, 183
Division Street, 194
Dixon, Mrs Henry, 33
Dolphin, Mr and Mrs, 156
Dow, Alfred, 52
Drill Hall, 54
Driver, Jack, 110
Duke Street, 174
Dundas Road, 66
Dunlop Street, 183
Dunn, Alderman E., 1

Ebenezer Wesleyan Reform
    Chapel, 23
Edgar Allen and Co., 17
Edison Swan Electric Light Co., 9
Eason, Mrs G., 185
Eason, Stewart, 185
Eastgrove Road, 63
Eastwood, Lt Gen T.R., 47
Eccleshall Road, 78, 179
Eccleshall Road South, 30
Effingham Road, Attercliffe, 124
Effingham Road Gas Works, 146
Effingham Street, 43
Ellesmere Road, 95, 125
Emergency Committee, 2–4, 8–9,
    18, 21, 42, 53, 61, 65, 84, 87–8,
    90, 93–5, 98, 126, 130, 141–2, 148
Empire Theatre, 74–5
Endcliffe Crescent, 180
Endcliffe Grange, 180
Endcliffe Park, 102, 178, 195–6

English Steel Corporation, 11, 17
Evans, Mr and Mrs J., 158
Exchange Street, 110, 193

Falding, Edna, 174
Farfield Road, 189
Fargate, 108, 124, 159, 171, 191
Finlay Street, 60
Fir Vale Centre, 34–5, 51, 142,
    153, 160
Firth, Col Mark, 21, 51, 53–5
Firth Park, 99
Firth Vickers, 17
Fitzalan Square, 77, 126
Fleming, J.L., 44
Fleur de Lis Club, 108–109,
    171–2
Foster, Margaret, 30
Foster, Rev J.E., 30
Fox, Connie, 32–3
Fox, Rev G.S., 33
Fox Street, 130
France, Aircraftman H., 23
Furniss, Audrey, 31

Garner, PC, 123
Gascoigne, Mr T., 158
Gibson, Mr E.B., 95
Gillott, Billy, 183
Glossop Road, 91, 130, 159, 193
Grant, Sir Allen, 155–6
Gratton, Dorothy, 113
Graham, Mrs L.E., 118
Grand Hotel, 162
Graves, J.G. Ltd., Crookes, 117
Greaves Street, Walkley, 79–80
Gregory, Mr, 80
Greenwood, Harry, 127
Greenwood, Joseph 127
Greenwood, Mr and Mrs A., 127
Griffiths, Mr A.B., 53
Griffiths, Will, 179
Griffiths, Maj W.H., 13
Grimesthorpe Road, 94

Hadfield Steel Works Ltd., 11, 114
Hall, Annie, 117

Hall, Maj B.P., 184
Hall, Muriel, 64
Hallet, Gloria, 26–9, 35–6, 66, 74, 93, 109–10
Hartley Brook Road School, 109
Hawksworth, Beatrice, 99
Haynes, Arthur, 180
Heeley, Barbara, 100
Heeley, Mr and Mrs, 100
Hemper Lane, Greenhill, 76
Hepworth, George, 62
Heys, Mr J., 53
Hickory, Mr E.H., 113–14
High Hazel Park, 195
High Storrs Grammar School, 81, 171
High Street, 77, 111, 159, 188, 191
Hill, Jessie, 98–9
Hillsborough Park, 195
Hobbs, Helen Gertrude, 122
Hodgson, Jim, 181
Hodgson Street, 26
Holly Street, 51
Hoult, Kathleen, 116
Hounsfield Road, 193
Howson, Col W., 51
Hughes, Mr V.M., 146–7
Hunloke, Lady Anne, 115
Hunter, Alderman W.J., 11–12, 15
Hunter, Dr L.S., Bishop of Sheffield, 81, 191
Hunters Bar, 98
Hurlfield Avenue, 52
Hutchinson, Barrie, 100
Hutchinson, Mr and Mrs M., 100
Hutchinson, Patricia, 100

Jackson, Brian, 180
James, Maj F.S., 119–28, 130, 158, 173
Jepson Road, Wincobank, 59
Jessop's Hospital for Women, 168
Johnson, George, 156
Jones, Douglas, 60
Judd, PC, 124

Kedie, Arthur, 91
Kerford, Edward, 74–5
Kerford, Nora Dorothy, 75
King Edward Grammar School, 29
King's Head Hotel, 91, 110
Kirton Road, 94

Ladybower Reservoir, 26, 159
Laking, Mr and Mrs, 153
Lawrence, George H., 80–1
Laycock Engineering Co., 168
Leigh Street, 52
Leger, Henry, 124
Lockwood, Mr A.P., 74
Lodge Moor Hospital, 191
Lodge Moor, PoW Camp, 137, 109, 191
London Road, 112
Longden, Alderman J.A., 41, 102, 108, 126
Longley Park, 195
Lowe, Mr G.S., 131–40, 175–6
Lydgate Hall Crescent, 44

MacKenzie, Lt Col A.F., 49
MacKenzie, Mrs, 49, 51, 55
Main Road, Darnell, 122
Maltravers Terrace, 74
Mallison, Mr and Mrs, 81
Manchester Road, 91, 159, 180
Mappin Art Gallery, 88
Marlow, Miss C., 71
Marlow, Mr and Mrs C.G., 190
Marples Hotel, 77–9, 89
Marples, Mrs R.C., 107, 142
Marshall, John E., 94
Marshall, Cllr S.H., 53
Massara, Luigi, 162
Matthews Lane, 62
Maud Maxfield School for the Deaf, 29
McCauley, Margaret, 27
McIntyre, Rev H., 30
McLardy, James, 99
McNerlan, Mr William, 180
McWilliams, Mrs, 168

Melling, Mr T.W., 114–15
'Mi Amigo', 176–82
Middleton, Keith, 95–6
Middleton, Mrs, 95
Millhouses Park, 51, 195
Milner, Cllr Luther F., 47–8, 82, 84, 151
Milner, Mrs Lucy, 147
Mitchell, Bernard, 162
Mitchell, Cllr C.J., 165
Morrison, Herbert, 131–2, 140, 162–4
Monks, Mrs A., 66–7
Moor, the, 54, 187, 191
Moore, Mrs F.R.S., 103
Moore Street, 186
Mortomley Lane, High Green, 138
Morton, L/Cpl Alan, 183
Mount, Spr George D., 17–18
Mylnhurst Road, Eccleshall, 33

Napier Street, 39
Neepsend Gas Works, 146
Neill, Col F.A., 39–41, 45–7, 50–1, 53–5, 193
Neill Road, 78
Nelson, A.J., 33
Nelson, Mrs, 33
Nether Edge Hospital, 34, 97–8
Newall, Mrs Rachel, 114
Newton, H.S., 24, 28
Norfolk Street, 144
Norman, Bernard, 162
Norman, Carol, 162
Norris Road, 174
Norton Cemetery, 83
Norton Grange, 62
Norton Lane, 33
Nunnery Colliery, 65, 83

Oak Street, 113
Oakwood Collegiate School, 30
Oldfield, J., 80
Old Town Hall, 20
Olivet Road, 111
Oval Hall, 167

Owlerton Sports Stadium, 51
Oxford Street Methodist Church, 144

Page Hall Road, Firth Park, 99
Palace Cinema, 184
Pallett, W.G., 168
Paramore, Thomas, 84
Parker, Mr J.K., 44, 75, 79, 130
Parkwood Road, 189
Payne, Flt Sgt Clem, 179
Peacock, Alan, 25–6
Peel Street, Broomhill, 31
Perrett, Bdr M.D., 186
Petre Street, 25
Peveril Road, 183
Pilmer, PC Henry White, 130
Pinstone Street, 187–8, 190, 193
Pitsmoor Road, 130
Plunkett, Mr, 80
Porter Street, 45, 72, 74
Powell, 2 Lt S., 52

Queens Road, 195

Radford, PC Samuel, 127
Randall, Lizzie, 111
Rawlings, Mrs Fred, 153
Rayley, Mrs, 168
Reading, Richard William, 78
Redfearn, Sylvia, 74
Redmires Road, 58
Regent Picture House, 54
Ridgeway Road Feeding/Rest Centre, 107, 143
Ridley, Emily, 114
Riley, Edward, 78
Ringinglow Road, 84
Rivelin Bridge, 159
Roberts, Capt Clement, 3, 20, 95–6, 185, 194
Roberts, Mrs B., 105
Robinson, Audrey, 31
Robinson, Mr G.W., 94
Robinson, Kenneth, 94
Robinson Shirley, 31
Robinson, W.J. 194

Rockingham Street, 54, 74
Rogan, John, 153
Royal Hospital, 162
Ruffell, Rita, 164
Rutland Road, 61

Sampson, Miss, 161
Sanderson, Sgt Douglas, 186
Sanderson, Michael, 186
Sanderson, Mrs, 186
Sanderson, Valerie, 186
Sandford, Mr H.K., 95–6
Saul, Mildred, 104
School Road, 174
Scott Road, 94
Sedan Street, 99
Seed, Alec T., 27
Sharrow Vale Road, 20
Sheaf Street, 60, 159
Sheffield Chamber of Commerce, 101
Sheffield Club, 165
Sheffield Corporation, 11, 89, 143, 146
Sheffield Court House, 4, 121
Sheffield Education Committee, 7, 16, 18, 113
Sheffield Fire Brigade, 9, 101
Sheffield, HMS, 82
Sheffield High School, 26
Sheffield Home Guard, 40–55, 89, 134–7, 155, 165
Sheffield Methodist Church, 191
Sheffield Public Welfare Committee, 142
Sheffield Red Cross, 161
Sheffield Road, Tinsley, 66
Sheffield Royal Infirmary, 61
Sheffield Sea Cadet Corps, 190
Sheffield Town Hall, 13, 20, 41, 54–5, 126, 144, 151, 162, 165, 170, 185, 187, 190–3, 195
Sheffield University, 39–40, 108
Sheffield Watch Committee, 21, 172
Sheaf Street, 159
Shrewsbury Hospital, 162

Sicey Avenue Rest Centre, 94–5, 144
Siddall, L/Cpl S., 52
Silver Hill Nurseries, Eccleshall, 116
Simms, Charles, 14, 87
Simpson, Margaret, 104–105, 112, 115–17
Skidmore, Mrs Joan, 186
Slayleigh Avenue, Fulwood, 93
Smith, Luther, 171
Smith, Percival Henry, 99
Southey Green Road, 107
Southey Hall Drive, 31
Spooner Road, Broomhill, 184
Springfield Road, 44
St Ann's Road Methodist Chapel, 153
St John's Ambulance Brigade, 91, 110, 193
St Luke's Church, 65
St Mary's Road, 75
St Michael's, Neepsend, 30
St Silas School, 26
Stainton Road, 179
Standon Road, Wincobank, 59, 69
Stansfield, Mr W., 148, 153
Staniforth Road, 123
Stannington, 34
Stephens, Fred, 26
Stevens, Geoffrey W., 31–2
Stevens, Rev R.C., 65
Stevenson, Barbara, 31
Stevenson, Earnest, 31
Stevenson, Ronnie, 31
Stokes, Cllr W.G. 80
Stone Grove, Broomhill, 180
Struan Road, 31
Surrey Street, 13, 187
Sullivan, Leonard, 73
Swales, J.K., 53

Tapton Bank, 83
Taylor, George, 79
Teather, Sup Int C., 9, 101
Tempest, Edna, 94

Thomas Firth and John Brown
 Ltd., 7, 21, 154, 188
Thorpe House Avenue, 83
Tinsley Park Colliery, 65

Union Street, 184
United Steel Company, 17
Uttley, Rifleman Albert, 183

Vernon, James, 131
Vernon, Johnny, 4
Vernon, Minnie, 130–1
Victoria Hall, 87
Victoria Station, 151
Viners Ltd., 17

Wade, Gladys, 184–5
Wadsley Bridge Rest Centre, 94
Walker, H.F., 16
Wallace, Rev William, 191–2
Waller, G., 80
Wallis, G., 96
Walton, Irene, 174
Warley Road, 66
Watson, H., 183
Watson, Phyllis, 174
Wentworth, Mr and Mrs J.W., 186
West Street, 13
Westbourne Road, 116
Western Bank, 193
Western Road, 44
Weston Park, 192
Weston Park Museum, 6
Wharncliffe Hospital, 34
Whitham Road, 91

Wicker Arches, 101
Wicker, the, 66
Wiggins, Staff Sgt W.H., 174
Wilkinson Street, 172
Willett, Brice, 113
Wilson, John, 153
Wilson, Thomas, 84
Wilson, Mr Thomas, 78
Wilson, Edith Grace, 78
Windle, Mrs J., 71
Wingerworth Avenue, Beauchief,
 168
Winslade, Edna, 60
Wisewood Avenue, 31
Women's Auxiliary Army Corps.,
 105–107
Women's Auxiliary Police Corps.,
 119, 131
Women's Home Defence Corps.,
 49, 51, 55
Women's Land Army, 115–16
Wood, Jean Mary, 33
Wood, Mr P., 83
Woodbourne Road Council
 School, 84
Woods, Mr W., 151
Woodsetts Road, 19
Woodward, Mrs Mary, 112
Woolley Wood Council School, 69
Woolley Wood Road, 69
Worthing Road, 64
Wortley Road, High Green, 138

Yarnell, Joan, 166